She Should Talk

Conversations with exceptional young women about life, dreams & success

ERICA EHM

HarperCollins*PublishersLtd*

SHE SHOULD TALK: CONVERSATIONS WITH EXCEPTIONAL YOUNG WOMEN ABOUT LIFE, DREAMS & SUCCESS

For information address HarperCollins Publishers Ltd,
Suite 2900, Hazelton Lanes, 55 Avenue Road,
Toronto, Canada M5R 3L2.

First Edition

Canadian Cataloguing in Publication Data

Main entry under title:
She should talk : conversations with exceptional young women about life, dreams & success

ISBN 0-00-638055-7

1. Women — Canada — Interviews.
2. Women — Employment — Canada — Interviews.
I. Ehm, Erica.

FC26.W6S54 1994 971.064'7'0922 C94-931578-8
F1034.3.A2S54 1994

---

94 95 96 97 98 99 ❖ HC 10 9 8 7 6 5 4 3 2 1

Printed and bound in the United States

for
bubby,
mindy
and my mother,
who taught me never to be afraid to ask

and for
tim,
steve
and my father,
who shower me with unconditional love and inspiration

Contents

Contents

Acknowledgments

This book started with an idea and a phone call from Maya Mavjee in November 1993. A huge thank you to Maya, my editor, who offered me a little dream and helped me see it through.

My mother, Evelyn Hannon, was very much part of putting this book together, co-ordinating and brainstorming. To her, a big thanks for offering perceptive insight, precious time and love. I couldn't have done it without you, mom!

Thank you to the HarperCollins team that has guided me through the process of putting a book together: Iris Skeoch, Judy Brunsek, Jane Rowland, Jill Lambert, Neil Erickson and Richard Bingham.

A big hug to Debra Thier for the beautiful cover photo and for being a great house-sitter; to Neil Graham for the studio and expertise; Kelly Jackson for the tasteful makeup; and Kalander on College Street in Toronto for letting us intrude and shoot there. A tip of the hat to all the other photographers who generously allowed their photos to be reproduced in this book.

When I was offered the chance to put a book together, I consulted several people who steered me in the right direction. Thank you to Catherine Bush and Nigel Hunt, Guy "Purple Prose" Lawson, Daniel Richler and Michael Coren for the generous advice. Thanks to Kim Zayak for taking the time to play with words. Also, many thanks to my multi-talented attorney, Colleen Wilson, who helped me with all legal concerns.

To my extended family at MuchMusic, who put up with me taking on yet another outside project and graciously worked around my schedule: Nancy Oliver, Denise Donlon, Moses Znaimer, Ron Waters, Suzie Kent, Margaret Weinrich-Perotta, Bill Bobek, Scott and Greg in security, all the producers and crews. Much appreciated!

Thanks to Shashi Iyer and Barbara Sloan at UNICEF, and all the UNICEF supporters I met across the country, for reminding me that I can make a difference.

Big kisses to my talented girlfriends who were so supportive and excited about this project, and whose strengths were inspiration for this book: Kim Stockwood, Larissa Lapchinski, Natalie Richard, Victoria James, Megan Oldfield, Diane Kerbil and Judith Hayman.

And most importantly, a huge hug, kiss and thank you for all the women featured in this book. It was such a pleasure having the opportunity to get to know each of you and to listen while you shared your strengths, your fears and your dreams with me. Hopefully, all of our voices together will make a difference to the lives of some young women who have their own big dreams. Thanks for talking!

She Should Talk

I was hungry and all I could think of was a medium pizza with extra cheese. I was ten years old. I gave my mom that 'I'm ready for dinner' look and suggested that she phone my favorite pizza delivery place.

My mother stopped me dead in my tracks when she announced that the time had come for me to learn to phone the restaurant myself. Panic seized me. Call a complete stranger? Just like that? What if they laughed and hung up on me? My mother looked me in the eye and explained that if I wanted pizza that badly, I'd have to work up the courage and make the call. Dinner was in my hands. 'Don't be afraid to ask,' she said. 'The worst thing that could happen is that they'll say no.' When she put it that way, coupled with my grumbling stomach, I grabbed the phone and 45 minutes later I was proudly devouring the first meal I ever had the courage to order all by myself.

Seven years later I was hanging out at a concert with my girlfriends when I spotted the program director for the biggest rock radio station in town. I was completely into music, spinning records at my college radio station. Before I knew it, those fateful words my mom had ingrained in my brain began to surface and my feet brought me face to face with this music-business big shot. I introduced myself, explained that we had previously met through my school and that it would be the best thing in the world for me to work at his radio station, and did he think it was possible for me to have a job. I guess I took him by surprise, because he let this overly enthusiastic 17-year-old be the station's official music librarian. Okay, so it wasn't a paying gig, but I had landed my very first job in the big-time music biz. Considering my distinct lack of experience, the main reason I must have been given this great opportunity was because I had the confidence to go up and ask. I learned that in this big, scary world that's chock full of potential, no one's going to come up to you and offer you some incredibly big break. You have to take the initiative, and the first step is having the nerve to ask for what you want.

Asking questions is what led me to this book. The art of interviewing is one of the tricks of the trade I've continued to develop while working in music television for the last ten years. As glamorous as rock'n' roll TV may appear, the job itself is demanding. The working environment at MuchMusic is best described as 'sink or swim,' and after several years close to drowning, I began to understand the medium of television. The tough part of the process for me was knowing that a large portion of the country was watching as I was learning my profession. Eventually I was able to address a camera as if it were an old friend. The ability to improvise on live television has become second nature to me now. Through trial and error, I figured out how to put together a flattering on-camera wardrobe, achieving a look that defies the dreaded curse of the camera, which notoriously adds ten pounds to even the thinnest television personality.

On the most basic level, my job at MuchMusic is simply to entertain and inform viewers across Canada about what's going on in the music scene. I have access to interesting information and insight about rock stars, the latest 'poop,' so to speak. In a medium that is constantly bombarding us with information, the tough part is to pass on the facts in a way that will continue to grab the audience's attention. What a lot of people don't realize is that once the daily show is over, my job isn't. By virtue of my very public career choice, aspiring rock journalists and on-camera hopefuls often look to me, and other on-air talent at Much-Music, for inspiration and guidance. It's our responsibility to share the experiences and knowledge we've accumulated on the job and pass it on to the next generation.

The ten women in this book are all in the same position of passing on some of their own wealth of experiences. Each of them, like myself, has had a dream of accomplishing a specific goal, be it in the arts, science or business. Through hard work, determination, tough times and talent, we're all making our dreams come to life. Many of the women I've interviewed are not usually in the public eye. By agreeing to be part of this book, each of them is acknowledging the fact that they, through their successes and sacrifices, have become female role models. Their motives for exposing themselves in these interviews were often to have the opportunity to describe their frequently difficult day-to-day lives, in the hopes of inspiring the same kind of strength and ambition in others who are ready for life's challenges.

All the women who chose to tell their stories on these pages deserve respect for having accomplished what they set out to do. But when you get right down to it, they're all just regular gals trying to get a break. It's no secret that, as we approach the 21st century, growing up is becoming more complicated. Coming from a broken home is commonplace. Drugs and guns in high schools are a problem. Educational standards seem to be slowly slipping. Jobs are more difficult to find. Yet even facing these kinds of odds, I easily tracked down these women who are managing to make the world work for them. What separates them from others who can't seem to get a break? There doesn't seem to be a magic formula, only common sense, a willingness to work hard and a strong desire to achieve.

Lately the media has latched onto the snappy 'Generation X' catch phrase to describe the post-baby boomers, which is the age group all the women in this book fall into. According to the buzz on

Generation X, those who belong in this category are known as 'Xers,' 'slackers' and 'the twenty-nothings.' They're described as being cynical and apathetic. They shun success because they believe that all the good stuff is taken, that they will never have the same financial comfort that their parents enjoyed. Some even go so far as to describe the young people of today as the 'lost generation.'

I'm not buying it. The point that seems to be forgotten amidst the rush to legitimize this new cultural movement is that the same thing has been happening for generations. Case in point—*Rebel Without A Cause*, the classic film from the 1950s. It's a natural reaction for young people to feel rebellious, disassociated and ignored by the mainstream. Growing up is difficult, no matter what decade you were born in. Now, though, through the power of the media, the concept of the slacker generation is being blown out of proportion. What those marketing geniuses who are trying to sell magazines aren't writing about are all the enthusiastic, daring and intelligent young people who don't fit the Xer description. Apparently good news doesn't sell well.

If you look around at what is happening in youth culture today, you will notice that this generation is particularly savvy. While critics scream and yell about the evils of television, the once-evil box also provides non-stop information that has allowed young people to see more of the world without leaving their own neighborhood. Kids growing up in rural parts of the country now have equal access to popular culture, thanks to modern technology. Computers, Internet, e-mail and modems make acquiring information fast, painless and fun. Some young people are being exposed to more ideas than their parents ever were. And this can lead to bigger dreams.

One inspiring aspect of putting this book together was the caliber and diversity of women's career choices. These days, the hot topic of conversation is the fact that we're growing up in an era of economic depression, and that there are fewer jobs for the taking. I was recently in Cape Breton, which has a dangerously high unemployment rate. I had been invited to talk with high school students about staying in school. When the floor was opened up for questions, one girl raised her hand and said, 'If there are so few jobs, why should I bother to stay in school?' The answer seemed so obvious to me. I guess it's all in the way you choose to see the world: as a glass half empty or half full. I explained that is exactly why you absolutely must finish school. If there are fewer jobs, then you're going to have to be one of the best at what you do to make it. Standards are higher, but the opportunities are there. Just be prepared to work for them.

And then there was the woman who attended a talk I gave at a college in North Bay. She stood up and asked what many up-and-coming broadcast students like to know. 'How did you get your job?' I gave her a quick rundown of all the different jobs I had taken since I was 17, all the way from my days as a volunteer music librarian at the radio station, working at record stores, DJing at clubs, to getting my university degree in communications, then landing the job answering the phones for Citytv's 'New Music' in Toronto, volunteering at the Maclean Hunter programming channel to finally landing my job on the air at MuchMusic. Her response? 'Isn't there a shortcut?' I wish I could have said yes, but the answer unfortunately, is no.

Because this book is about celebrating the accomplishments of women, we cannot take for granted that a book like this could not have been possible in my parents' generation. Today Kim Reid is flying F-18 fighter jets. Ann Duggan is a doctor in Azerbaijan. Nathalie Karvonen opened up the Toronto Wildlife Centre. And Alison Reid is one of Canada's top stunt performers. When my mother was 18 years old, she was expected to get married as soon as possible to a man who could financially support her while she raised their loving children. The problem wasn't having a husband and raising a family. The frustration stemmed from the fact that this was all that a woman was expected, or allowed, to do with her life. A job and financial independence didn't mix with marriage. And if a woman was lucky enough to be hired as a secretary or waitress, she would be paid a fraction of what a man would earn doing the exact same job. This was only 25 years ago.

Not long ago I was part of an informal gathering of women at a friend's house. Twenty women were invited. Their ages ranged from late 30s to early 50s. Most of them were professional women with children. I was by far the youngest. Discussions ranged from how to get ahead in the arts community to how to make your bread rise. Eventually the topic of feminism snuck into the conversation, but I couldn't relate to their interpretation of what feminism meant. They used it as a muted battle cry, as well as a password to a strong sisterhood. For me, the concept was passé. I took my independence and career for granted. But as I looked around the room, it struck me that these women were responsible for doing a lot of the dirty work for me. They were the ones who read *The Feminine Mystique*, and were compelled to take action to change attitudes. They were the generation of women who had to fight for equality both in the home and at work, who protested for the right to be treated as equals. I'm a product of their success. Thanks to my feminist mother, I've been brought up to assume that men and women are equal. I take it for granted that I can work to support myself and have a family if I choose to. But it's no coincidence that all the young women who were interviewed for this book felt uncomfortable labeling themselves feminists.

The women of our generation are being referred to as 'daughters of feminism.' We're going places our mothers' generation only dreamt of. Imagine their pride watching their daughters become the women they wished they could be. But for us, feminism brings to mind extremists, man-haters and self-righteousness. This kind of attitude isn't as necessary these days. Many battles have already been won. This is not to say that all is peachy keen in the wonderful world of being a woman. According to statistics, it still isn't equal pay for equal work yet, but it is getting closer. There are more women who hold powerful positions, but not nearly as many as men. Sexual harassment is rampant. And back at home, a woman is still expected to take care of the family, even though she, like her husband, has a full-time job.

On the bright side, there are more women who have been educated and trained to deal with these problems. Our standards and expectations are higher than the previous generation's. We are a demanding bunch. When you read each of the women's stories featured in this book, it will strike you how driven and hard-working they are. They don't take no for an answer. Their work is their hobby. Their lifestyles are often controversial. They've all made some kind of sacrifices in their lives to achieve their success. Today's young women have come to expect that we deserve what's rightfully ours. Life is for the taking.

She Should Talk

Alison Reid

Imagine being thrown down a flight of stairs, hit head-on by a speeding vehicle or set on fire as a way to make a living. For Alison Reid, it's all in a day's work. At 29 years old and only 114 pounds, Alison has become one of Canada's most respected stunt performers.

Raised on a farm near Newcastle, Ontario, Alison grew up a tomboy, running free in the wide open spaces. Although she always had a daring streak, nothing could have prepared her mother when Alison announced that she was taking a private course to become a stuntperson. It came as a bit of blow when, years later, her mom realized that Alison was deadly serious about breaking into one of the most dangerous occupations there is. Every one of Alison's successful stunts allows her mother to breathe a little easier.

Alison and her boyfriend, Bryan Renfro, now live in a beautiful home in a rural suburb of Toronto that has been paid for by their long list of stunts. It's mainly in the thriving Toronto film and television scene that she's racked up her impressive résumé. She's worked on

120 major productions, including *Deathwish V*, 'My Secret Identity,' 'Tekwar,' *Black Robe*, 'Street Legal,' *Police Academy I*, *III* and *IV*, 'ENG,' '21 Jump Street' and 'Road to Avonlea,' to name just a few. Once Alison established herself as a dependable stunt performer, she decided to try giving the orders instead of following them by taking on the responsibility of stunt co-ordinator. When she's not on set falling, crashing, burning or co-ordinating, Alison is probably speaking out on equality at the Women's ACTRA Committee or talking about accident prevention as the chair of ACTRA's Health and Safety Committee.

For a professional whose very way of life is outsmarting danger, safety is a huge concern—it's the difference between an exhilarating stunt and the catastrophic loss of life. As a matter of fact, when I arrived to do my interview with Alison, her head and hands were still bandaged because of the second-degree burns she had received when a series of explosions misfired on a film set. She showed me the footage of the accident. All you see is Alison and then a blinding flash of light, and then Alison running towards the camera—on fire.

I listened in disbelief and horror as she recounted her stories of near-death misses. And even when she wasn't getting blown up, the videotapes of her many successful stunts still made me squirm. I looked at this tiny (size six) ball of fire recount these exploits and noticed that she was smiling. Was it pride? Or was it because she's a survivor, she's lucky and she knows it? Or was she just reliving the thrill of her stunts? No matter what was actually going through her head, it was apparent to me that in a profession dominated by men, Alison defies the stereotype that it takes muscleman brawn to do a 'man's job.' A strong woman with brains and guts is equal to any task.

I always wondered what it is in certain individuals that makes them thrill-seekers. According to Alison, there is a chemical condition that separates those who live for a thrill from those who avoid it at any and all cost. And so it happened on a Tuesday afternoon that two women, who belong on the opposite ends of the thrill-seeking spectrum, embarked on a roller coaster of a conversation.

When I was coming here to do this interview, I was warned that you were suffering from second-degree burns. What happened?

An accident I had about a month ago. There was a shot in the movie where I was supposed to be running away from a building, and there were eight explosions that were supposed to go off behind me. Somehow, the wires crossed so that when the button was pushed, the whole lot went off and I was right in the middle of it. I was very lucky to get off as lightly as I did. Let me show you a couple of pictures.

Oh my God! Your face is completely swollen! I wouldn't have known it was the same person. What went through your mind when you heard all these simultaneous explosions?

The instant it went off, I thought, 'Oh shit'—that's exactly what I thought. And I was mad because it should never have happened. There was just a big, big flash and the next thing I remember, I was out of it and both of us, the other stunt guy and I, fell down. I don't know why I got up and just kept on going with the action, running through like it was planned. The stunt co-ordinator, as I ran past him, grabbed my wig and ripped it off my head because there was nothing left of it. It just disintegrated, and my pants were on fire for a bit too—they were nylon so they just melted. I remember thinking when it went off, 'Are we going to be lucky and come through this or is it going to be real bad?' I didn't know how much flame we had to go through to get out. I was most concerned about my vision because it wasn't right for the first little while. Luckily that's come back, and the only permanent damage is going to be a pigment change on my forehead, which is quite disturbing. I didn't think I was that concerned about the way I looked until this happened but I'm sort of freaking out about it now.

But then you get to wear your war wounds with pride. Was this your first big accident?

Unfortunately not. I thought I was safe for a while because I've been doing this for 12 years and I'd say this is my third serious one.

Sometimes you can go for years and, you know, just get your normal bumps and bruises and scrapes and stuff. Last year I was rolling a car and the roll cage caved in. It wasn't constructed properly so I got a compression fracture. I fractured my neck—my C1 vertebrae. That was a very close call.

And you're smiling. That's what's so interesting.

Well what else can you do? You've got to feel lucky, right? Very lucky.

You also get to tell these great stories.

Yeah, well, now I'm developing a guideline to do with roll cages because we haven't got stats. We have the technology to build safe roll cages, but it's not just a matter of welding a couple of bars in a car. You really have to get the experts to do specialty things like cages.

I was talking to a producer yesterday, telling him about this accident, and he said, 'Alison, what did I tell you after that last one—you're too small, you're too frail to be doing this kind of work.' And you know, it's like, I don't care if it's Arnold Schwarzenegger in this frigging car—if you've got a car coming down on your head, you're going to break. And I get other people saying, 'Alison, it's a good thing you're so strong and you're so fit or else you never would have come through this stuff' and I think the same thing. I think, 'Man, I don't care if you're as strong as Arnold Schwarzenegger, you know, you're gonna break.' Being fit and agile is going to help you out in certain situations, and help you bounce back from injuries faster, but it won't make you super human. So it's just luck. When stuff like that happens, it's just luck whether you come out of it or not.

What is it in you that tries to defy death?

Well, I don't try and defy it, I don't think.

You did it twice already. You defied it. You blew up in an explosion. You rolled a car and you survived it. That, I would say, is defying death.

Yeah, but that's not what I set out to do. We set out to do these things extremely safely. These are screw-ups—major ones—but normally, things are set up so that we're not defying death, we're outsmarting it. It's only when you don't take into consideration something that you should have, or someone screws up, that you're in real jeopardy. The problem with doing stunts is that a lot of times, you're very dependent on other people, you're dependent on other performers and you're very dependent on special-effects people. The trouble is, everyone's human, and sometimes they make mistakes and that's when you get hurt.

What happens in an event like that, when someone screws up? Any hands slapped?

Well, accidents shake everyone up. No one likes accidents on the set, especially producers, because safety records are very important for insurance as well as the human toll. I think it's more important to analyze why an accident happened and make sure it never happens again rather than slapping hands—but sure, it happens.

I think these photographs of you with your burns are going to haunt me.

Yeah. They look like special effects. I went into my bank and they thought it was makeup—that I was just popping in off a movie set. It wasn't until they looked really closely that they saw it was real.

I ride horses. There are times when I get thrown and I don't want to get back on. I think that if I was riding a horse and I fractured my neck, I don't think I'd get back on. Why do you?

I had exactly the same reaction after my first accident. I was really spooked. You know, we're used to taking the knocks—getting hurt and getting back on. But I remember lying there in the hospital with a fractured neck, they told me to be absolutely still, and I remember just wiggling my toes and my fingers to make sure that I still could and thinking, 'You're so lucky, you could just as easily be lying here not being able to do that.' And I told all my friends that I really had to have a re-evaluation of my life because this wasn't worth it. I mean, I love doing stunts, I really do, but I love my life too. And then I got over it. You know, time goes by, and you're talking to stunt people and talking about stuff that's going on. I was off for five months and by the end of that five months I was just itching to get back to it. This time I'm having the same reaction. I'm thinking this is permanent damage. Every day from now on, when I get up and look in the mirror, I'm going to have a reminder of this.

You're looking at a woman who can't go on a ride at Disney World because the sensation is so awful for me.

Well, you know what it is—I did some research into this. There's a spectrum of people, and some of us are called sensation-seekers. It's a biochemical thing and there are different ways sensation-seekers get their little buzz. Some of us are physical, some of us are social sensation-seekers and there are others who don't find any of it comfortable at all. It's to do with all these enzymes and neurotransmitters in your brain.

Why did you do this research?

Because I was interested in it myself. When I was at Ryerson, my roommate and I did a documentary called *Thrills*. We interviewed some thrill-seekers and a psychologist who explained a bit about why some people really need that sensation. I know I really do, unfortunately.

What kinds of stunts do you do?

I could be doing something as simple as sitting in a car, not even driving it, but just being a passenger in a fast car. Or I've doubled for Carol Burnett sitting in a helicopter. You know, everyone's so freaked out about the *Twilight Zone* helicopter crash that you just don't want to put an actor in that situation. Or it could be an uncomfortable situation, like maybe it's really cold and the actress is wearing a skimpy wardrobe and she can only be out there for so many takes, so they put you in there for the wider takes. Something like that, all the way up to the fire gags, high falls, car hits and the stair falls.

When you do the stair falls, or the jumping out of the eighth-storey windows, you can't help but hurt yourself, right? Even if you do it properly.

Oh yeah—you're absolutely right. Those are the stunts that we call 'hardballing it'—where you know you're going to get banged up and you pad as well as you can, but when you're falling down a fire escape—fire escapes are the worst because they've got metal edges and sure, you're going to take a shot here and there. It's part of the game.

So explain to me how one trains to be a stuntperson. I know you went to Ryerson Polytechnic in Toronto.

Yes, but I was doing stunts a long time before I went to Ryerson. I sort of don't know why I went to Ryerson. I guess I felt I needed more education. I left school when I was 17 to pursue stunt work and finished high school by correspondence. But my actual stunt training was through a stunt co-ordinator, which was the best way to get trained. There are a lot of fly-by-night stunt schools that come and go, but they're not usually run by professional stunt people, and are not a good way to break into the business. I was trained by a stunt co-ordinator. The film business was just picking up in Toronto and there was a need at that time for stunt people, so he taught me the basics—like the basic fight moves, how to move, how to fall, the function of how to fall off a bicycle or down some stairs or out of a car, that kind of stuff. It's very important to know how to do that. So he got me started on high falls and the car stunts—the 180s and the broadsides.

Isn't it sort of an odd choice for a 17-year-old girl to decide she wants to be a stuntwoman? When did you first realize you had this desire?

I can't remember when the idea first struck me, but I remember wanting to be one for quite a while before I actually pursued it. It was the only thing I really wanted to do. I was thinking, 'What would I really like to do? I'd like to fall out of buildings for a living.' I liked to be thrilled. I don't like monotony. I was really sick of school at that time. Of course, I have a different perspective on stunt work now that I'm actually in it. There's a lot of...oh, everyone pictures that every minute you're doing something absolutely thrilling, whereas what happens is, you go in in the morning, you go through makeup, you go through wardrobe, you go to craft services, you have a snack, you wait around for ten or 12 hours. That's the way the normal day goes. There's a lot of hanging around going on, which drives some people nuts.

Hurry up and wait.

Exactly.

What is a stunt rodent? I think that's the funniest term.

I don't know who came up with it, but there are always a lot of people who are sort of intrigued with the stunt field and they're trying like crazy to get in. Obviously there is a stunt community and they're tried and true performers, and a stunt co-ordinator would have to be crazy not to hire those people first. These are the people who're good at it and making their living at it. They're the professionals and you're going to hire them. But there are always these stunt rodents, as we call them, who are always hanging on, trying to break in. And everyone's got to do that at some point, so that's just a little term we use when they get annoying.

You were a stunt rodent when you were first learning. How did you go from learning how to do it to actually getting paid to do it? Someone had to have some kind of faith in you to think you could handle it.

A stunt came up—in *The Littlest Hobo*—12 years ago now.

How old were you?

Oh, 17 or 18.

What did you have to do?

Oh, it was a nothing stunt. A cake day, you know. We call those days Jesse James days, because you're kind of stealing the money. There's an earthquake in a cave, so the character gets trapped in a cave—we shot it in a studio. They had a fake cave made up and I had a bunch of Styrofoam boulders and peat moss fall down on me and that was that.

Not very dangerous.

Not at all. I wish you could predict the dangerous things, though.

This explosion stunt that I got hurt on, I wasn't the slightest bit worried about it, not the slightest bit. It was, like, no danger at all. So you can't always predict those things. Sometimes it's the little ones that get you.

Tell me, is it pretty new to have women as stuntperformers?

Stuntwomen have been around for a long time. What happened more in the early days was that guys would dress up as women and do the stunts. And I'm not pleased to tell you, but this still happens today. Although it doesn't happen very much, and I've been quite outspoken on several occasions when it's happened up here, because we're at a stage where there are quite a few stuntwomen, capable stuntwomen. There are situations that arise where you will have to cross the sexes. I've doubled guys, but it's been for good reasons. Like there isn't a guy my size with my skills who can do this particular job. And that's the only reason a guy should double for a woman. If there isn't a woman around who can, you know, jump 16 cars on a motorcycle—if there isn't one, then it's okay for a guy to fill in and do it. There's still the odd stunt co-ordinator who wants to put the money in his own pocket, especially on the bigger stunts, so he'll do the stunt himself. That's not a legitimate reason with me at all. Our union has rules about it. Anti-discrimination, equal-opportunity clauses, and through the Toronto ACTRA Women's Committee, I've got some more specific clauses in the Independent Production Agreement.

Why are there so few stuntwomen? I was reading that there are about ten across the country. Is that true?

Depends on how loosely you use the term stuntwoman. There are some stuntwomen who toy with it. There are very few who are professional—who make their living at it.

Why is that?

Well, partly because there's less of a demand for stuntwomen than stuntmen. There are far more stunts for men, just the same as there are far more acting roles for them, and I guess that fewer women want to do it than men.

What were your parents' reactions when you threw yourself into this work?

My mother thought it was a phase, I think, and that I would grow out of it. She's very good though—I know she worries a lot. She's never been to see a stunt. She's been on set a couple of times, but only when I've been co-ordinating. She'd rather know about it when it's all over and she knows everything's all right. I hated calling her and telling her about this accident. I didn't call her for a few days after my neck accident. It's a hard thing to say.

What did you say?

'Remember that car roll I did last week?' I tried to word it as delicately as possible. 'It turns out I've got a little fracture in my vertebrae.' 'Oh yes—are you wearing a neck brace?' she said. 'Oh no, actually I have this contraption bolted into my skull.' And the burn—my sister's a dentist and her boyfriend's a doctor, so they came down to the hospital and I said, 'Don't tell Mom, don't tell Mom,' and my sister said, 'Alison, you tell Mom, because I can't not tell her.' I would have liked to have waited a few days, because I knew she'd want to come and see me, and of course she did, and I was looking my worst. I opened the door a crack and said, 'It'll go down, it'll get better.'

How did she react when she saw you?

Well, I had prepared her well, you know, she's good that way. She doesn't let her feelings get in the way of what I want to do. That's probably the reason we get along so well.

And what about your Dad?

They broke up when I was 17 or 18.

So it's really you and your Mom?

Yes, and my partner Bryan and my sister and her boyfriend.

When you go on set and you're preparing for a stunt, say your eighty-foot jump out of the window—your average eight-storey jump out of the window—is there a sort of physical warm-up that you have to do beforehand?

To tell you the truth, I don't. Not for a high fall. If you want to run or something like that or you can stretch a little bit and warm up your muscles—but for the high fall, no.

What about getting burned? I mean, enveloped in flames?

It's not really physical, it's more to do with wardrobe. The protective chemicals and clothing that you put on underneath your actual wardrobe, and also the flammable stuff that they put on top of you. You're really dependent on people to prep you for a fire gag—and to put you out.

It's interesting that it's called a fire 'gag' as if it's something funny.

We call a lot of the stunts 'gags.' I don't know where that comes from.

One of the stunts that you're known for is being engulfed in flames. When they light you on fire and you're standing there, engulfed in flames, what goes through your mind?

The first thing that goes through your mind is—honest to God, 'Am I on fire?' Sometimes you have to look and make sure you're on fire. Then you're just trying to move around and do whatever action you're supposed to do—do your routine like you've rehearsed for the scene. Sometimes play with the flame...make it look real. If you get hot...start to feel hot spots, then you have to go down on the ground and your safety people come and put you out, because the minute you feel hot, it's going to get worse, and very quickly.

When it gets hot, what's not working properly?

I don't know—sometimes you just get a hot spot here and there. Usually it's in a place you can't protect very well—the edges of your ears. We have a substance called water gel that we put on exposed skin. That allows you to put your hand or your face in it for a little while—a very little while. And areas like the edges of your ears always seem to get burned because it's very hard to keep the gel on them.

You've also said that you like the sensation of falling, which again, to me, is the worst thing in the world. Say

you're doing your biggest fall, what's going through your mind? Before you take off and then as you're falling?

The actual fall happens so fast—but before—I've been through every extreme doing high falls, from being totally comfortable to being totally scared. I like heights, but everyone's got an innate fear of heights. In one picture, this person's actually supposed to be committing suicide and what happens is someone catches them. So I'm standing there and I've got a rope attached to my back or a wire or something, but I'm actually standing on this ledge on the top of a building and I have to jump off and there's no air bag down there. You can't see an air bag. It's a total headtrip. It's not physically dangerous, because I've got safeties on and I'm going to be fine. But I was up there and it had been a while since I'd done any high stuff, and my legs were just quivering. I was standing up there going 'Oooohoooh.' Then 'Action' is called.

You just have to overcome that fear for one split second while you jump. If you're actually doing a fall, then you're concentrating on flailing a bit to make it look exciting, and you're also judging when to flip over. You land on your back and the best position to land in is totally out flat. And if you miscalculate that—if you under-rotate or over-rotate—you get hurt. But you want to leave it as long as possible to turn over so they get the longest fall, because the fall's over once you turn over. That's basically an instinct thing. You don't really think about it, you're just reacting.

Do you like the actual feeling of your stomach dropping out?

But that doesn't happen. It's not like a roller coaster when you fall. It's not like when you go over a hill or something and your stomach falls—that doesn't happen—there's no movement like that. You just fall.

What about mental preparation?

It depends very much on the stunt. I think the most important thing when you're heading into a stunt is to be totally confident that you can do it. You cannot have a fraction of a little inkling of thinking 'Oh, I'm going to get hurt.' You have to go into it totally confidently. For instance, in a car hit. A car hit is when you get hit by a car. There was one where I was standing in the middle of the road, firing a gun, and this car's coming straight at me and the driver broadsides me and takes me out with his trunk. Normally the car just hits you head-on and you roll up over the hood and that's it. No matter which way the car's going to hit you, your timing is so critical. If you're too early or too late, or if your body isn't in the right position, you're going to get seriously hurt. But you can't be thinking about that. You have to be thinking totally positively. Not that you're cocky about it, but you've got to have that positive attitude or else it's not good.

It'll obscure your judgement?

Yes.

Stunts are your job, but who you are allows you to do it. Who has had the biggest impact on your life?

My mother, definitely. Mothering is such a thankless job, and I wouldn't want to do it myself, but it's such an important job. What she did was instill in me the confidence to do whatever I wanted to do. I never ever thought, 'I can't be a stunt performer.' It never even crossed my mind. And that's just from growing up being totally supported, never having to worry about anything and being totally encouraged in whatever I wanted to do. That's the only way I can put it.

Were you a tomboy when you were growing up?

Oh yeah. I grew up on a farm and I used to ride horses too. Show jumping was my thing when I was growing up. Farm life is—you know, you're haying and fixing fences from cows that got out and stuff, and chopping firewood. I liked that a lot. You're taught responsibility. You're taught about life. You see animals die, we used to nurse animals. We were city people who moved to the country. So you learn about life.

It seems to me that you're doing what you've always wanted to do. You're writing scripts, co-ordinating stunts and you're

on three different committees to track the way women are treated in the stunt world. Why are you so powerful inside?

A certain amount of it is just going for it. I think it's very rare that someone grows up without a lot of scarring or something that inhibits them somehow. But what's the worst that can happen? Just going for it and not stopping. That first script I sold—I went in—you know, the advantage of working in stunts is that everyone in the film industry tends to know you, so you can just walk in. I did this about ten times, I'd written about ten different outlines, and it was no, no, no, and finally I said, 'Screw this, I'm writing an entire script,' and they said, 'We'd like to buy the story, but we'd like someone else to re-write it'—and they wouldn't give me a shot at re-writing it. It's very hard when you haven't got a track record. And then the next year Bryan came up with a great story idea, so I wrote the teleplay and handed it in. This time they let me do it. So it's not being discouraged by the no's as well. You just have to keep on plugging.

Do you feel there's a need to test yourself all the time? To push yourself farther and farther, and try more difficult things? Put yourself in difficult situations?

Yes, I find I need to push myself. Not necessarily as far as stunts go. I like it when a bigger stunt comes up, because it's much more exhilarating to go in there and roll a car than going in and falling off a bicycle, but that's not up to you. So I challenge myself more in the coordinating and writing areas. On a day-to-day basis, I push myself in my workouts. I have to ride the Life Cycle at a certain level for a certain length of time, or do a certain amount of weights, and that's the thing I want to be doing more of and not let myself slide physically.

Okay. So what level?

Seven — well, actually, I'm just getting back up to seven because I've been off with this accident.

And how long do you cycle?

45.

45 minutes!

Yes—it's nothing too wild. I tend to Life Cycle a lot because my third accident—which I haven't told you about yet—destroyed my knee. I've had tons of reconstructive surgery on it and I've another one booked. But I've got to the point where I can't run outside any more. It tends to bug my leg. We have a treadmill downstairs that I ran on for a while, but I can't even do that any more. So swimming and Life Cycle and weights are what I do to keep fit.

You're beating your body up.

I know, and it worries me, because I respect it and I want it to last, and I don't want any more accidents, that's for sure.

I'll second that. When it comes to your profession what was your biggest mistake?

Okay, here's one mistake—something that I used to never, ever do and that I now realize gets you respect as a stunt performer—saying no. Because there are two types of directors. There's one type who's very safety-conscious and very willing to listen to you telling him or her what is possible in the situation. Most directors are like that, but there's another type who has this picture in their head of what they want and they'll do practically anything to get it. They need to be told, 'No, this is all I can give in this situation.' When I wrecked my knee, I was riding a Harley Davidson and we were shooting a chase scene. I was racing a Corvette around a very tight corner, a very, very tight corner. We shot it a couple of times and the director kept saying, 'Faster, I want it faster,' and I was doing it as fast as I could, given the corner. And you know, it's in us to want to do the best job we can possibly do to please him, rather than saying—which I would say now—'Undercrank your camera and it will look faster.' I said, 'Okay, let me see how fast I can do it.' Luckily the cameras weren't rolling and I went into the corner real fast and hit the guard rail and destroyed my knee. Didn't destroy it, but it's not going to be the same again. So knowing your limits, knowing what's usable and sticking to it, you get respect for that. Whenever there's an accident, you want to downplay it, because accidents get blown out of proportion very easily. So I got up and took off my helmet and I'm walking around and I knew my knee had been hit pretty badly, but I didn't want to say anything, and there was an ambulance there and everyone runs over, and I say, 'I'm fine, fine,' but then I finally went over to the ambulance and said, 'Okay, I'll get this checked out.' And I was wearing Spandex pants and I said, 'I'm fine really—I just want to check out this knee.' I rolled up the pants and there's this little scrape on my knee and I thought, 'How disappointing!' I mean, I really thought this knee had been demolished. So I took down these Spandex pants and there's this great gaping hole and all the meat's hanging out, and the ambulance guys plunked the oxygen on me and took me to the hospital and I got stitched up. Now here's the thing. There was a guy hanging around who's an excellent motorcycle racer—far better on a motorcycle than I am. So they throw the wig on him and get him to do it. Here I am, pulling for women to do these things, and now I screw up, have an accident, and now a guy's going to get on the motorcycle and do it right. It pissed me right off. So I came back to the set and I'm driving another car on set now. I've got stitches in my knee. I'm driving the car ahead of the action. And I look in my rear-view mirror. We're still shooting this damned corner, and I see him sliding across the ground on his ass (he was okay, he just got some road rash), so I thought, 'Yeah! Now they've got to know they're asking too much.' And that made me happy.

So you've learned that if something doesn't feel right, even in your day-to-day life, you have to put your foot down and say no. People will respect you.

Absolutely. And as a co-ordinator, that's even more important. Because it's not just Alison you're responsible for, but a lot of times for other stunt performers and actors too. Sometimes an actor, who's very physical and able, will want to do a shot and you'll be fighting them. You're dealing with an actor here. If they get hurt, you've got no show. So sometimes you have to say, 'No, sorry, I can't let you do this.'

From what I understand, it's even more dangerous sometimes to be doing stunts as a woman—you can't wear as much padding because the clothing is smaller.

Yes. Costume designers don't always take into consideration the things the stunt performer is going to have to do. For instance, I've been asked to jump from building to building in high heels—you'd break your ankle for sure. Or fall down stairs in a mini skirt, so you can't pad your knees or whatever else you need to pad. Asked to do car hits in skirts. Guys get to wear pants most of the time.

What role do politics play in your life?

I'm the easiest-going person in the world, but when there's something that's not right, I can't help it, I have to open my big trap. And the trouble with doing that in this business is you're totally dependent on people to hire you. A lot of people who you may disagree with on certain issues are the people in hiring positions, so there are stunt co-ordinators, maybe just a couple, who won't go near me because I've spoken out. There are some people who play the politics really well, but I'm not one of them. I just say what I think.

Let's look into the future, if your daughter comes to you and says, 'Guess what, Ma, I'm going to become a stunt woman like you,' what would your reaction be?

First of all, I have to stretch my imagination. It's hard to picture that mother thing.

Okay then, a niece. A young woman who you really love.

Well, okay. I'd tell her the same thing that I'd probably tell anyone who is thinking about it. And ironically, the night I got burned, there was a young guy on the set, about 18 or 19, who wanted to do stunts and I told him, 'If you do this business'—and I didn't know I was going to get hurt that night—'you're going to get hurt. Sooner or later you're going to get hurt.' If you had interviewed me a few years ago, I wouldn't have said that. I would have said, 'Oh we set up things very safely and you don't have to get hurt. You get bashed around a bit, but you don't have to get seriously hurt.' But that can be a very high price to pay. There are a lot of things I've loved about doing stunts. I've had days like this where all I do is work out, do whatever I want to do. When you get a call to go into work it's a great feeling—you're not dragging your feet going in there. You love it because you don't get to work every day. I love the business. There are some real positives about it. There are some prices to pay sometimes. On the whole, you should have something else that you can do as well, so you can have the freedom to say, 'No, I don't think I want to do that car stunt.' What you have to do is follow your heart. If it's in someone's heart to do it, they have to go for it and do it. If someone had told me, way back when, and I'm sure they did, 'You're going to get hurt,' well, it's a good thing to keep in the back of your mind, but it's not going to stop you.

What's the right reason to do stunts or to become a stunt performer?

Just that. Because you want to do it—you need to do it—you want it with a passion. You won't make it as a stunt performer unless you have that inside you.

Do you see yourself as a role model?

I've never thought of it. I guess, like that kid—he didn't know who I was when he first started talking to me, and then he went, 'Oh, you're Alison Reid, oh wow.' I guess some people look at me that way, but I don't go around thinking that I am one.

But you are, in a sense, setting an example for young women.

I am. There are a lot of examples these days. Like Roberta Bondar, (the astronaut) who everyone can look up to. When someone has a dream and they pursue it.

In your spare time, for fun, you skydive.

I have skydived, but I don't do it any more. My insurance doesn't cover me for it. And I have hang-glided, but I haven't flown lately. I rock-climb still—I really like rock climbing—but no, on a day-to-day basis what I do is I work out.

These things that you sometimes do for fun, like hang-gliding, parachuting—which to me are all terrifying, death-defying—to me it says that you're afraid of very little, and I wonder what *are* you afraid of?

I get really nervous doing interviews on television. They scare me to death. I don't know why, but that scares me.

So I'm afraid of what you're doing and you're afraid of what I'm doing—we're even.

We'll trade some day.

No way!

Jennifer Fournier

So many young girls have dreams of growing up to be beautiful, long-legged prima ballerinas. Some girls try to turn their dreams into reality by taking ballet classes. After a few years of *pliés* and pointe shoes, some lose interest, while others are physically unable to keep up with the increasingly demanding pace and choreography. Very few actually end up making ballet their life.

When Jennifer Fournier was just four years old, she knew that she wanted to dance the rest of her life. Even at that young age, dancing was what made her feel truly alive. Twenty-one years have passed and that drive and desire have never left her.

At four, dancing with innocent abandon, Jennifer was beginning her difficult journey to the National Ballet of Canada. At 12 years old, after eight years of ballet class, she was one of the few who passed the National Ballet School's notoriously difficult general audition. This meant that she would have to move away from her family in Ottawa to board at the ballet school's Toronto headquarters. The sacrifices Jennifer would have to make for the rest of her career had begun.

The school is tough. Standards are high, both academically and in the dance studio. Discipline and devotion drive the dancers. Pain becomes familiar as they push their bodies harder every day. Dance becomes all-consuming. After five years with the ballet school, Jennifer, along with only two other graduating students, was invited to become a full company member of the prestigious National Ballet of Canada. And that's when the real work began.

Now, at the age of 25, Jennifer has just been promoted to first soloist, making her one of the company's rising stars. She is one of prima ballerina Karen Kain's favorite young dancers. When she's on stage, she becomes the picture of elegance. Her precise movements are graceful and polished, the living embodiment of the traditional feminine beauty that little girls dream about. As well as a natural physical ability, it's ultimately Jennifer's pragmatism, ambition and need for perfection that have allowed her to achieve this level of success.

When Jennifer opened the door to her downtown studio loft for me, I met a slender, long-legged woman with a little girl's turned up nose that crinkled when she giggled. Her body language was strong and self-assured as she sat comfortably in her sweatshirt and leggings on her second-hand sofa, her live-in boyfriend's abstract paintings all around us. Jennifer's driving ambition and intelligence were striking. Those qualities, as well as a refreshing sweetness, shone through that evening while I had the pleasure of talking with one of Canada's most talented ballerinas.

The first time I took in a ballet was one of your performances in *La Ronde*. You played the prostitute, the seductress with red hair. It was so interesting for me because I come from a background of pop culture, while what you do is ultimately classical. There's such a mystique about the cloistered life of a ballerina.

It's just the discipline involved in maintaining a tradition that's so old. There's something incredibly demanding about making ballets like *Giselle* and *Swan Lake*, and the technique itself. The technique and giving the ballets life. It requires so much focus and knowledge and discipline to get to that point where it becomes free, within such a rigid sort of set-up.

I guess that's where the art comes in.

Yeah. There's a very specific structure in classic arts, and then the art comes in when you can find the magic within that very strict structure.

When do you see someone dance and say, 'That's a great dancer'?

When I feel like I'm watching someone who just has to dance. When I'm watching someone dance and it looks like it's a part of them—an intrinsic part of them—they are the dance. I don't see the separation. I don't see someone dance, I see the dance. It doesn't happen very often. There are performances I see—there are dancers who are beautiful, who have incredible line, exquisite quality, but when you see a dancer and you go, 'Wow, there's a dancer,' it's rare. And it's when something about them is just...necessary. You can't imagine them doing anything but dancing. There's not many of them, unfortunately, who allow themselves to get to that stage. There's something so Dionysian about dance, it's inexplicable, like a bacchanal, it's kind of a loss of self, so that your body is so informed on its own. You and your body somehow are working in an incredible way. To me it's such a freaky thing to witness. It's an inexplicable talent.

Ballet is a classical art. Are traditional values also encouraged in all the young dancers?

It's hard to say that. I don't think so. Because it's an artistic lifestyle, and because you're walking around all day in tights, leotards—practically naked in front of men and women—we tend to be more liberated with our bodies. I think dancers tend to be a little more liberated sexually. From a younger age. I remember that—I sensed that when I dated this guy who was not a dancer. I remember him being kind of shocked at me, because I was so—not prudish, but pristine and young. But sexually I thought quite freely—uninhibited, you know. And I think that's part of being a dancer. I really do. I think that any performing art tends to be a little looser—performers tend to be a little looser with their values and a little more open with their appreciation of other people's lifestyles. They can accept a lot more.

Tell me about your early ballet days.

When I was growing up, there was always music around the house. We always had a stereo—one of these chesterfield-looking stereos, you know, you'd open the top and there was the record player—all this space for this tiny little record, and we always had music on. And my mother brought me to ballets, *Coppélia*, *Swan Lake*. And then I would get the records—ballet music like Tchaikovsky's. We listened to 'Nadia's Theme' and The Carpenters and you name it, all sorts of stuff. I would sit in the living room—it's so clear to me, the level of involvement—it started off maybe once a week or I'd just be in the living room and dance around. At first it was just fun and then it became a deep, personal journey for me. I would shut all the doors and I would dance all around the room. I would become the character. And Coppélia dances to very little of the music, but I thought all the music was Coppélia's. So I would try to remember what she was doing when that music was on and I'd dance—everything from the mazurka, the czardas, create all these dances.

How old were you?

Five, six. I started at four. I remember some nights, I was older, nine, ten—I remember when I was still dancing around the living room and I would start to perspire—I was old enough to perspire—wear myself out dancing around the entire living room. Running around, doing all this improv. It must have been hysterical to look at. I wish I had a videotape, I really do. It was wild. But there's no question that was the only thing I was completely taken with. I'd just listen to music all the time. I always had music on. Music is a big part of my life—has always been.

And then you started taking ballet lessons when you were how old?

Particularly bad ballet lessons when I was four, and then...

Are there good ballet lessons for four-year-olds?

No, but I mean, I'm saying it wasn't anything like—it was in this big gymnasium. But it was beautiful, being a butterfly, exactly like you imagine it to be. There are pictures of me downstairs in my parent's basement in these silly little ballet costumes and I had a huge stomach—I was so chubby—my hair in this big bun. I went to another dance school after that and then another, sort of less bad school. And finally I went to a pretty good school when I was ten and then the National Ballet school when I was 12.

In order to get into the National Ballet School you had to audition. What do they look for?

I think they look for—I'm assuming now, based on what I would look for—a good body, obviously, you have to have a certain amount of rotation in your hips, long tendons, a nice jump, good proportions—that's part of having a good body—no heavy curvature in the spine, and then ideally, things like arched feet, long legs, short torso—I have a short torso, that's one thing that's ideal—long arms, long neck, small, round head—that's the ideal.

Twelve years old and you accepted a scholarship to the National Ballet to train in Toronto. You were living in Ottawa at the time. That must have had a huge effect on you, leaving your mom and dad, your sister.

Yes, it did. I think it was really hard on my mother, because somehow when you're 12—it was close enough that I didn't feel I was going halfway across the country. And I was working so hard in Ottawa. Basically, I spent all my time dancing. I was at school all day and then I would go straight to ballet class. It was so exhausting. I would get home late and then try to do my homework. In a lot of ways I was leaning in that direction. I could go to National Ballet School and that would be a fulfillment, or I wouldn't be accepted and that would be a crushing disappointment. So when I was accepted, it was a very positive thing, and I'd never really thought about—oh, I have to leave home. For some reason I just went. It was hard, but I went. But I know it was harder on my mother. In retrospect, you know, I can't believe how hard it must have been for her, if I try to imagine losing a daughter. I missed home, but you know, me and my sister, we fought. It wasn't a depressing thing. I know some people have such a hard time going, but for me, when I feel like something is necessary—or it's at least going to take me closer to something I want—it's a sacrifice I'm happy to make.

By the time you were 12 years old, you virtually had given your life to ballet. Tell me about the training required.

What's hard about it is the repetition. Because in ballet it's not enough for your mind to know it, your body has to know it. Your mind can understand what a *plié* is, or what you're after on a double *plié* to the back, but your body has to do it over and over and over before you master the simple things. Before they become part of your muscle memory. I never thought so when I was young, but I realize it now, just from seeing how long it takes me to change some habits, that I have a very quick mind but I have slow muscle memory. It takes me a while. I have to do things quite a while before they're ingrained in me physically. Just the same exercises, every day, forever, until the end of your career. Like you do in class. Like you have to do *pliés* and *dégagés*, every day.

Even now?

Yes.

So when you were going to school, what was your normal day like?

Well, usually, I think this was in Grade 10 or around there, every day at nine o'clock we'd have ballet class—nine to 10:30, an hour and a half. And then we'd have 15 minutes to get changed and then we'd have our school and we'd do 45-minute periods of English, math, and then we'd have another ballet class, say four to 6:30. Then 6:30 to eight, we'd have maybe *pas de deux*. Finish the day, go have dinner and then do your homework. There were sacrifices. Certain things I would have liked to take, but I finished in Grade 12. I don't feel like I got quite the education I would have gotten if I'd gone to a private girls' school or to a public school. Just the incredible variety of things you can take in a high school. But at the same time I have to qualify all this by saying the level of training, the level of my class in particular, was incredibly high, because in general the girls—not so much the guys—but the girls who end up in ballet are driven generally. The standard of academics is very high. We all kind of pushed each other, we all wanted to write long essays on complicated topics. When I think back on it, if it wasn't for how disciplined we were in school, we probably wouldn't have done what we did.

Because the focus is on your body?

There comes a point where, in Grade 11, all of a sudden you know there are certain girls and boys who are going to go somewhere, whether it's the National Ballet of Canada or somewhere else. But they're the upper echelon. And the priority becomes dance. You can only last until 30 or 40 and you've got to make hay while the sun shines. So you've got to be in there dancing as much as you can, rehearsing for shows. If you need a rehearsal at three o'clock for *Swan Lake* and there's a French class, you go rehearse. When we were doing shows and we were working really hard, we didn't have to do the homework that other people had to do—there was a certain amount of slack, definitely.

Who's had a major influence on your life?

At different times it's been different people. When I was young, when I really look at myself objectively as a young girl, I was incredibly driven, just by myself. Really driven. When I look back to some of the things I used to do when I was young, sometimes I can't believe it. It's not like the person I am now. I was so driven to pursue success — not money, just excellence. When I was at the National Ballet School, it was other dancers, others so far above me that I aspired to dance like. It wasn't until I was 17 or 18 that my emphasis became less on that kind of thing and more on people. Qualities in people that didn't have to do with outright success. Just what made them gracious, and thoughtful. And that was definitely something that came later for me. I would say my mother—just so gracious and so warm. And my father, definitely my father's integrity—work ethic. Industriousness, too. My mother had that, too. There's Karen Kain, who has inspired me. She has been for me one of the few role models who has been consistent, from my youth to now, she's still there. She personifies so many of the best qualities that a ballerina could ever have. Intelligent—very intelligent. But also instinctive and very generous with all of her artistry and very gracious and humble and, with all the success she's had, very modest. She's been very lucky, but she sees her good fortune and she's an incredible person. And also, recently, Magdalena Popa, she's a coach in the company who—without her, I couldn't have gone nearly as far, personally or technically. Not many people know about her because she's very much behind the scenes, but she's like a genius—the best coach in all the world.

What's the relationship like between a coach and a dancer?

Oh, it's so important. Maybe some dancers don't need that, but to achieve real greatness I believe you have to have a coach that you trust. There are psychological aspects to it. Often a coach will see—with Magdalena, she takes a different approach based on whoever she's working with. And with me, she knows that I am very disciplined and that I need to feel prepared, and I don't have a huge amount of confidence in myself, and she knows I need to do things over and over, and she drives me to do them. Some people get intimidated by the fact that I'm a perfectionist and they say, 'Oh chill out, chill out, do it once and that's that.' But she's the opposite. She makes me do it over and over and over so I know, I believe, I can do it. She's amazing. She works with everybody differently, but she gets the best out of people. Seriously, without her, they wouldn't happen. She's an unsung hero.

And now you've just sung her praises.

Well, she deserves it.

You've been described as a young woman who doesn't rattle easily. Have you always been this really strong-willed person?

You know, it's so funny because I don't see myself like that at all.

Any more? Or like that ever?

You know, the past couple of years have been so hard. I think to myself, 'I can handle anything.' Except for a few things that could upset me. It's not a question of *if* I'll get through it, it's just *how* I'll get through it. Like, what I'll learn from it.

Very pragmatic.

I guess it is. That's my background I think. It's very Irish, isn't it. My family, on both sides, are real survivors.

When you say the last couple of years have been really tough, has it been in your dancing or because you lost your mom?

It was both. My mom—it was incredibly hard to deal with that. Watching someone you love die. I truly believe that part of me was with her, fighting it. But the slow realization and the exhausting battle.... I felt like I went through it like she did, except there was a switch somewhere where I felt like she was the child—probably the last four or five months of her life. It was just so painful. Part of me is relieved that it's over. Awful as that may sound, it's incredibly hard...on your spirit. To witness someone else's spirit be constantly beaten—constantly.

I would do anything to somehow turn back the time and switch it around. We all had so much optimism and she just astounded me with her faith. It was exhausting and at the same time—because it was really hard on me—she was my rock. And it was like—this is happening in my family. My family's always been so solid. It was weird. And then as well as that, I got injured. I had three injuries in the past three years. I broke my foot, right before the season where I was doing quite a bit. It would have been a very important season. Very slowly I practiced rotation and the next season I was all ready to go and I sprained my ankle on stage the night before opening night. I was really frustrated. I came back for the last week of the season, but I wasn't fearless because I had just sprained my ankle. And then I did *Nutcracker* again and got ready for last season. Last February, I was doing some other really great stuff—you know, I'm getting to the age where now I feel I have really good shows in me, because I feel things are coming together, the technique and the artistry. I wanted to accomplish something on stage. And then, my back went into spasm. I've never had back problems, but my back was just like—I couldn't move it. I missed the entire season—the entire February season. It was such a blow.

This is at the same time that your mother was...

Yes, just at the time, that season, that my mother was on her downward...

So there must be some emotional connection.

Yes, but at the time I couldn't accept it, because I wanted to be on the stage so badly. It was a psychological thing I'm sure, the back. The foot wasn't—it was a fluke.

What happened?

It was just an accident in the studio. But it made me so angry because it didn't have to happen. And it happened at a time when I'd just made a breakthrough, prior to that, and technically I was in good shape. It was hard. A very bitter pill to swallow.

It's also an incredible time to grow, because something's been taken away from you that means so much to you. You know you can have it back, you know there's hope, but it's going to take some time. You're given this time and it's your choice what you're going to do with it. You can waste it or you can really make something out of it. Your career's so short that time off from dance, no matter how aggravating it can be, is so precious. Usually you never have time off, you never have time to think. I did stuff that I had never done. And from the first injury I came back feeling really good. I was very clear about what I wanted to do. I don't like to mess around, I don't like to—more so after the injuries. I was driven before, now I'm a little more systematic about how I work. You just don't have time to waste.

I remember hearing a few months ago you got up and you made the most unbelievable eulogy for your mom, even though it was an emotional earthquake for you.

Well, it was so hard. The night before, I was up all night crying and trying to write notes down. Couldn't even think straight. Things would come into mind—it's like when you walk into a room and you're asked to describe it when you leave it and you can't. Or even your apartment—you just can't. It's too close somehow. And it was the same thing with my mom. Later on, as the months went by, I thought of some things, qualities of hers, and I wanted to save them. I wanted to get up and—I wanted one of us to say something because I don't think anybody felt able to do it. I'd been a real mess that day, I remember, because it was three days later and that's when it really starts to hit you, so I was crying and up all night and—then that morning, I woke up and it was like—okay. I knew I had to say something and I just couldn't let myself get upset. It was the last day of the open casket and we had to go and...you know, the last farewell. I couldn't let myself get tied into that kind of emotion or I wouldn't be able to say anything. I don't know where it came from because I was just a mess up until that point. I was probably the worst.

It was like the performer in you kicked in or something.

Yeah—totally. I wanted to do it. It very much was a performer's instinct. To control it, bring it all in, get grounded, take a deep breath, and all that you know is that people are there, the show must go on. I tried to think about things about her that made me so happy. I don't know how I did it.

The art of ballet works against your natural body, so aren't you in physical pain a lot?

You know, right now—of course when I'm injured I have pain—but I'm usually pretty pain-free. I'm very lucky. Because I work really intelligently—I don't have a lot of bad habits. I try to be aware. I don't like to take drugs, I don't like to anesthetize myself.

Is that a common thing?

Well, that's what people take to kill pain and I don't like to do that because I like to feel what I'm feeling. If it gets really bad, I'll take them. So I have that sort of safety valve if things get really bad.

Do you ever get used to the pain? It becomes a way of life, doesn't it?

When I'm exhausted, I'm so happy. When I'm working on stuff that I love and I'm exhausted, I love that feeling. Just coming home and relaxing. The physical exhaustion and the mental exhaustion....When you're doing something like *Romeo and Juliet*—I could work with that forever and ever and ever. But the flip side is when you're doing stuff you don't really love—that's kind of exhausting and that can be hard, it can be physically abusive.

You know you're not up there at the front, but it's physically demanding and in some ways it's more abusive, because you're on stage all the time, standing on the side, and you've got to rehearse endlessly and all of you are doing the exact same thing and that's exhausting, it's really hard. Those first years in the company when I was doing a lot of corps, it was tough, very tough.

What happens when dancers are injured when they're young, like your partner?

It's incredibly difficult. I had another friend who had a knee problem and was operated on twice and said, 'It's not going to work.' She'd been dancing her whole life. It's very cruel. She basically had to spend the next couple of years slowly trying to put together an idea for herself separate from being a dancer. Because it becomes a part of how you see yourself. Your self-image. Any performer—it's not so much the adulation, it's just doing it. It's a very spiritual thing—it's a lot like meditation. It's hard to find that involvement. That's why a lot of dancers often turn to spirituality. I think if people tell you that you should go to school and find something else for yourself, they're lying to themselves. It's not that easy. For most people I've seen who have left, it's a very long road to feeling whole again.

The image of a ballerina is the ultimate in femininity, yet the qualities needed to become a ballerina, like perseverance—physical strength and ambition—are more traditionally associated with masculinity.

It's a real difficult issue in the dance world. It is very much the case. You've got to know what you want. You've got to be—not pushy, but you've got to be, to some extent, very sure of yourself. It's a very rare woman who does have those feminine qualities and who was raised that way. There are a lot of women who have gotten to the top who weren't aggressive but who were really talented. They have people who sort of usher them up there. But if you run into problems—let's say you run into people who aren't crazy about your dancing, because it's a very, very subjective art form. You're always relying on someone else to give you roles. You don't go, 'Okay, well, I'm going to do *Swan Lake* next year.' That's what's so frustrating about it. You've got to be smart. If you're not going to do what you want to do, there comes a point where you ask yourself, 'Do I want a career, do I want to be the dancer that I think I can be?'

How does feminism fit in your life?

Well, I mean, for me it's so rarely an issue because I'm in a world that glorifies women. Dance is really a glorification of a woman and all her feminine qualities. I would say it's hard to have to constantly battle my body in terms of my weight—even just keeping your weight ten pounds under, that's a huge battle. Feminism really is an issue of freedom, right? My problem with lack of freedom doesn't stem from being a woman but being an artist in a country where the arts are not enough a part of the fabric of our society, and that's when I feel angry and deprived.

Tell me about the ballerina's battles with weight.

Well when I was 11 or maybe ten, my teacher in Ottawa said to me, 'You're going to have a weight problem, I can tell by the pot you have there. I don't want you to lose weight, but just watch yourself, don't gain too much weight.' I guess because my sisters were heavy, they were afraid I was going to end up like that. But how do you say that to an 11-year-old and not have some effect? I started dieting at the age of 11. It was very off-and-on dieting, and you slow your metabolism down. You start dieting at a certain age and, I don't care what anybody says, every time you have to start dieting again, you have to eat less and less and less. Until your body becomes so efficient you have to basically eat nothing in order to lose weight. Or else work incredibly hard. I go to the Y—I don't want to get out the violins or anything, but it's really hard. You have to make a commitment, you have to decide, because often it's the one thing that could stand between you and being the ideal. It comes so easily for some people. If I didn't have to worry about it, I think my life would be incredible.

You have to be thin so you look beautiful on stage?

It's the line, it gives you a quality of lightness you can't achieve when you're overweight. There are overweight dancers who are absolutely incomparable. You can still be great, but it's better to be thin.

When my friends and I go to the ballet, we watch all these lovely ballerinas on stage who are tall and very thin. Do you think it affects those of us who have average weights?

Well, I know when I went to New York this summer, I was overweight—from my holidays—yes, I was, I was overweight.

What is overweight? What does it mean?

Michael, my boyfriend, was kind of surprised when he saw me. He was, like, 'Oooh honey!'

So you were overweight...how much?

You know, we rarely weigh ourselves. You can just tell, you can feel it. I remember I went and saw City Ballet and I was just sitting there like—I was happy because I was watching a wonderful dance. But it was really hard to see the parade of skeletal—well, I didn't think of them as skeletal—incredibly beautiful women all night. By the end of the night I felt like a real jerk. And then I went out and had something to eat. I definitely have insight into that. It must be very hard. But it's no different than opening a fashion magazine, really. Except people on stage are working hard—the people in fashion magazines aren't. But I know it's difficult. It sends a funny message.

Do you think the emphasis on a ballerina to be thin is perpetuating a certain standard of what beautiful is?

But it's the nature of dance. There are certain standards, certain ideals, and when you're working in an office you have certain standards, too, that may seem inhumane. Maybe it stems from productivity or certain abilities that I can't understand. A 150-pound woman in a tutu—it just doesn't work—or a leotard for that matter, or pink tights. It would be great if it worked—in a perfect world, maybe it would—but it just doesn't. Guys can't lift them—you can't see the line. When a body is streamlined, you can see all the movement, because the body has equal value. You don't have these huge thighs that draw your attention.

Or big breasts that keep shaking every time you move. It's distracting—it is. It's very sexual, and it's more comforting to some people to see these women in these tights when they're kind of androgynous. It can get kind of strange when you see a very womanly woman running around stage in a leotard. If you're overweight, you just don't get on stage that much.

How are the expectations different for the female dancers and the male dancers in the company?

Oh, it's *so* different. Oh God! So different. In general, men rise more quickly because there's less competition for the men—less men dancing and.... Our company has a lot of talented male dancers. You can be a principal dancer if you're a man and have certain qualities, like being an incredible partner or an incredible jumper or turn quite well. But female dancers, to get to the top, always have to have everything—body, technical ability, the artistic ability. They've got to be able to interpret, they've got to be intelligent. Usually they have to be beautiful in some way. Not classical beauty like a model, but beautiful to look at, usually. And it's harder because there are so many more women. The standards are higher. This is not to say there aren't male dancers who are not as incredible, but you have to have more. You can never, never relax. There's always some little girl, five years younger than you, who can do everything you can and who's five years younger. People like someone new—let's see what she can do. Isn't she lovely? Look at that, and it's her first time on stage. It's exciting. For dancers, you get to that awkward middle stage. You've been around for a while, you're not a bona fide ballerina like Karen Kain, you're not the new kid on the block, you're like yesterday's news. You have to be doing something very special for people to stay interested in you.

And where are you in that category?

I'm kind of in the middle, you know. I'm new in the principal roles. I just did my first *Romeo and Juliet* and I just did my first *Coppélia* and for me that's really exciting, but in terms of the scheme of the company, I'm not a young kid. There are kids younger than me and I definitely feel the heat. You see why it's very much a youth-oriented business.

How do opportunities compare for older male and female dancers?

Men don't last. Men's careers don't last as long as women's. Because it's so physical, it's so athletic, what they have to do. And if, let's say, they do more partnering roles? Chances are their back is going to give out. It's a harsh truth, but it's pretty much true.

When I asked how feminism fit in your life, you said you see yourself more as an artist than a woman. What kind of sacrifices do you have to make as an artist?

The financial sacrifice is enormous. The instability worries me. When I think about what I'm going to do when my career's over in less than 20 years—it'll be over in 15 years probably, hopefully. It's not that easy to stay living in the city of Toronto, making what I'm making. I think that's an enormous sacrifice and it's one, obviously, I'm prepared to make, but as I get older I make it more and more grudgingly, because I feel like what I do is worth a little more than I'm paid. If I could do what I wanted when I was 40, I should be able to have a kid, raise a family and I wouldn't have to worry about getting a job. That bothers me. It's a huge sacrifice, especially if you decide that you're going to make it. I don't know if I'm going to make that sacrifice. Make that sacrifice not to have a child. Even if you do have a child, it's really tricky working it in. And ballerinas with children are not that popular.

Why?

Oh, it's just kind of unspoken. People's impression of you changes when you have a child. It's really true.

Because you're not giving 100 per cent of yourself to your art any more?

You're not dying for it—you're not ready to die for it. You've got other responsibilities that come first. Same as getting married. It's not said, it's not spoken. But there aren't that many women who have children anyway, you know.

Are you happiest on stage?

I'm pretty happy on stage—sometimes. I'm happiest on stage when I just let myself go and stop worrying and stop trying to be perfect. But in the studio, it's the opposite, because the quest for perfection is so exhilarating in the studio. You have this time and you can work on something until you get it perfect, just the way you want it to be. And that's so exciting, to be able to work on something and see it improve and be in control of your environment. On stage you can't be—that can't be your primary objective, to be in complete control. Because you'll just be disappointed. I think that being on stage—it's so exciting when you can let yourself go and decide to see what happens, but believe in yourself. Really give everything—all the positive energy you have—and some amazing things happen. It can't compare to anything—the lights, the people, the audience, the energy.

What's the best advice that you were ever given?

Just do what you want to do. Do what makes me happy. Because I've a tendency not to do that sometimes.

You tend to do what's right, what's expected?

Unfortunately, yes.

And what's the best advice that you would pass on to someone? Who is a dancer or not.

I would say, have a certain level of integrity about what you do. If you have ethics about what you do, whatever it is, then you'll always believe in what you do. You'll always feel it's right. You'll always stand up for it, even when it's not appreciated. It's something so—is ephemeral the word?—in dance, getting to the top is so ephemeral, you never really feel secure, you never feel, 'I'm here and I really deserve it.' If you know that you have ideals and standards and you maintain them, you can always feel good about what you do.

When do you feel, or do you ever feel, like you're grown up?

Yes, I felt it the night I found out my mom was sick. Well, you have to grow up. It was trial by fire. You can come out of an experience like that and not have grown up, but I can't imagine how. I knew that, as soon as it happened.... I'd had a kind of fantasy, fairy-tale youth. I was 21 and it was, like, time to enter the real world—sadness and, you know. Not everything was going to be the way you thought it was going to be.

Now, let's gaze into the crystal ball, your daughter that you're going to have when you're 40 years old wants to be a ballerina.

No.

You wouldn't encourage her?

Well, if she wants to. Oh, if my mother had stood in my way, I can't imagine how upset I'd have been, but oh, it's so—in so many ways, I'm one of the lucky ones. I'm getting to do it and getting paid for it and I get to do quite a bit, I'm quite successful. But there's so much heartbreak along the way, and it's heartbreaking for me to see it. So much undeveloped talent and some kids that have the talent and maybe they just don't have that little piece that they need to make the passage. Of course, if she was like me and dancing around the living room, I wouldn't stand in her way.

Five years ago you were quoted as saying, 'Young dancers don't see themselves in clear perspective. I think that I'm a lot less talented than others think I am.' Today, you're a first soloist, you've far more experience and success, so how would you describe yourself now?

I think that I have more inside of me than even I realize sometimes. And perhaps I have more inside of me than others. Not so much physical talent, just more that is going to come out and that I want to come out, that I want to develop. If I'm given the right opportunities, if my growth is consistent, I know that I can develop into the artist I want to be. I hope that happens.

What's striking me now, after talking to you all this time, and despite all the tough things you've been through, is that you seem content.

Yes.

Comfortable with yourself.

Yes. I'm happy to be—I used to think sometimes I wanted to get to a certain point where I was the Big Man on Campus, when you get to be a principal or a soloist. I could never feel like that, and I realize now it's not me. I'm much happier with a sort of beginner mind set—always striving. I know what I know and no one can take that away from me and I have confidence in my knowledge. But I accept that I'll always want to go beyond that. I'll never feel like I've arrived or feel complacent. I see some kids sometimes do things that I just dream about—like multiple pirouettes—but I work on those things, and when I do them sometimes, I feel great. It's okay if I don't do them all the time. I don't have to feel like I'm the best.

Kim Reid

In those classic old photographs of pilots that date back to the early 20th century, all we ever see are handsome, mustached men sporting leather jackets and aviation goggles. But what about women?

This is not to say that women were banned from the cockpit. Amelia Earhart flew from Newfoundland to Ireland in 1932, becoming the first woman to make a solo trans-Atlantic flight. Almost 65 years later, Captain Kim Reid is continuing the process of breaking new ground for women in the air by flying one of the most prestigious and demanding of aircraft—the CF-18 jet fighter.

Since she was a girl growing up in Victoria, B.C., Kim Reid has had a passion to fly. She began learning when she was 14. The first step was joining the 89 Pacific Royal Canadian Air Cadet Squadron in Victoria, where she spent her time studying aircraft while socializing with kids who had the same aspirations. With the financial help of several scholarships, Kim spent the next couple of summers taking flying lessons, earning her glider's and then private pilot's license by the time she was 16. She was hooked.

Kim's dream was a big one. To become a commercial pilot was not challenging enough for her. After spending four years studying at Royal Roads Military College, Kim was accepted into what is essentially the "Top Guns" of the Canadian Air Force. Only those who finish in the top 30 per cent of the class, both on the ground and in the air, stand a chance of making the cut. Competition between students is intense. After a year posted in Moose Jaw, Kim proved to be one of the elite of the student pilots when she was chosen to fly fighter jets in Cold Lake, Alberta. Another year and a half of intense training and she was ecstatic to finally be posted to 441 Tactical Fighter Squadron.

Being a fighter pilot is extremely demanding, both physically and mentally. Because there is only one pilot per plane, the task load is high, with little or no margin for error. When you're flying at the speed of sound, precision and a quick mind are essential. A bad decision could mean the difference between life and death. There's also an incredible physical pressure in the cockpit that builds when travelling that fast, battling gravity. Even the best-trained pilot can black out from the G-force. It's dangerous, difficult and exhilarating.

Despite the thrill of her daily practice missions, Kim never loses sight of the fact that she is ultimately a trained soldier of the sky, who can at any time be sent to fight in a war in which Canada has agreed to participate.

Captain Kim Reid has had to fight long and hard to reach her goal. Her only disappointment is that, at this point, she's the only female in the Canadian Armed Forces flying CF-18s. It's her hope that, by taking the time to tell her story, she might inspire some young girl with a passion for planes to believe that one day she, too, could be breaking the speed of sound.

Initially, when we were trying to get together, you were going to borrow a jet to fly to Toronto for this interview. Is this like asking your parents to borrow the car for the weekend?

No, it's not. Sometimes if we have a specific reason to go somewhere, to fly a specific mission, I can couple that trip with something that I'd like to do, which is great.

What kind of a plane were you going to fly here?

The CF-18 Hornet.

One of the fighter planes. How fast do those things go?

If I were to come out and visit you, I would probably travel Mach 0.8, 0.9.

Now explain that in civilian terms.

In civilian terms I would say—oh, 800 miles per hour.

Do you travel at the speed of sound?

Sure! The CF-18 is capable of up to Mach 1.8. It takes up a lot of gas, but we can do it. However, we are restricted to less than the speed of sound because of the damaging effects of the shock wave. One can reach the speed of sound quicker as you climb. The higher you go, the colder the temperature and the speed of sound is reached at a lower airspeed as the air temperature decreases. This is why we measure our speed relative to the speed of sound.

So as an introduction to what you do, can you give me five character traits that a good fighter pilot should have?

This is going to sound strange, but one of the greatest is humility. To be a good fighter pilot, you have to make mistakes and learn from them. That means that you have to be able to take a lot of criticism. The greatest fighter pilots that I know are humble. They're good, but they've learned from everybody.

The second is strength of character and a desire to go forward and get things done. You can't sit on the back burner and have somebody else do things for you. Third, you have to be in shape. Fourth, you have to be able to get along with other people in a stressful environment. If you're a loner or if you don't like crowds, then you'll probably get picked on in the fighter pilot community. We are very good at eating our young. The last trait is being able to know when to speak and when to listen. That was one lesson I learned early.

So what prepared you for living and working pretty successfully in a virtually all-male environment? Do you have older brothers?

Oh yes, I sure do. I have two brothers; one older, Mike, and one younger, Chris. They picked on me constantly and I did the same to them. I was always a tomboy as a kid. I had dolls, but I had more fun playing with my brothers' planes and toys, so eventually I coerced my parents into buying me those toys instead.

What about your mom and your dad—are you more like your mom or your dad?

That's a good question. My mom is very academic, she's a very intelligent lady. My father is smart as well but as an electrician, he's also very good with his hands, especially intricate work. One could say that I'm a good cross between them.

You've chosen a very non-conventional profession for a woman. I wonder if your mom is a feminist, if this influenced your choice.

A feminist. That term was never really used in my household. I would say my mom was more of a humanist. That is to say she never said no to me and she was progressive with respect to human rights. She never said you can't do this because you're a woman, and that was very, very important, I think, because it put me in a positive mind set. Labeling my mom a feminist in the sense that she supports women's rights, I would say, yes, she is. There are different definitions of feminism, however, in my mind not all promote equality and working together

What is your definition of feminism?

Feminism to me includes human rights, equality and working together harmoniously. Labeling that definition as feminism is restrictive since I believe it should apply to all people, not just women. I find myself shying away from extremists of feminism. They do not represent who I am, or what I do and I feel they tend to isolate themselves from men instead of trying to work with them.

Let's go back to your parents again. What was the most powerful thing each one of them taught you?

I would say my mom taught me perseverance and my father taught me how to relax and enjoy life. He's always laughing, always smiling and very relaxed. Whenever I'm around him I feel at ease.

You know, at 14, most teenage girls are giggling about guys. You were busy learning how to fly, which is pretty unusual. Since no one in your family is a pilot, where did this interest in flying come from?

When I was a young girl, and as early as I can remember, I used to daydream a lot about being an astronaut or playing some sort of character with a hero role. I used to love doing that as a kid. When I turned 13, I saw an avenue to actually pursue something that excited me, so I said, 'Yes, that's me, let's just go for it.' I was very goal-oriented and it just felt right to do it. I saw myself becoming a pilot, getting a degree and eventually becoming an astronaut. That's what I saw when I was 13.

I'm assuming that your mental images of pilots and astronauts were men, because there weren't a lot of female pilots. Is that true?

I guess I looked forward and I recognized that eventually there would be women doing these things.

Did you ever have a role model?

Maybe a fictional character. Waldo Pepper—do you remember that character? Robert Redford played a fighter pilot in this movie. He was this great pilot, fantastic hands and feet. He wasn't necessarily the most honest character in the movie, but I loved the way he flew and the way he was in control. This was something I aspired to do.

And what about a mentor, a person in your life who actually has had a huge influence on you within your profession?

Yes. Her name is Olivia Barr, she was my English teacher and councellor in high school and she's my great friend to this day. Whenever I have a problem, a concern or a question about where am I going in my career, I always give her a call and she always says something wise to steer me into line, which is wonderful.

How did she become your mentor?

Well, she was my English teacher and I trusted her. I went to her as a counsellor and said, 'I want to go to a military academy.' She just lit up because she thought it was a very good choice. She is, by my definition, a feminist as well. She took me under her wing and helped me with the applications and wrote a recommendation to help me attend the Royal Roads Military College. Since then, she's always been there for me, to talk about a number of issues: where do I want to end up in the military, or if I get out, do I want to do anything else, where could it lead me. We've talked about me as a female role model and what obligations I have with respect to that. This is all fairly recent as, up until I'd say a year ago, I never really felt I had the experience to be a valid role model. I felt I couldn't talk to anybody seriously about being a fighter pilot because in my mind, I wasn't a good enough fighter pilot yet.

A year ago, a lot of my friends and military colleagues said, 'Hey, Kim, go out and talk to some people, and get women interested in the fighter pilot world because this is a really great career.' That's something that I've discussed with Olivia and since then I've met and talked to air cadets and high-school students. Seeing their eyes light up is a pleasure. They're often surprised at what I do and it's a wonderful feeling to tell a 13-year-old girl, 'Yeah, you can do this.' It's a wonderful feeling.

So let's go back to you being quite young. Now, when you're learning how to fly, there are dual controls. Your teacher can correct any mistakes you make up in the air. What about that first solo flight? How old were you?

I was 16, and I was in a glider in Princeton, British Columbia. That was the summer of '83, I think.

Can you describe the feeling of being up there all alone?

It was fabulous. It was exactly where I wanted to be. I had a grin on my face the whole time, and I didn't want to come down, but being in a glider, you don't have an engine, so you can't stay up there forever. I was very proud of myself and I knew that it was what I wanted for my career.

Was there any nervousness?

Oh yeah! Definitely. I was definitely nervous. You have to rely on what your instructor taught you and say, 'Okay, I've got to remember all of this, I better not mess up.' Sure, there were nerves, but in some respects it makes you perform even better.

By the time you graduated from high school, you were certain you wanted to go to university and that you wanted to be a jet pilot. But why did you choose the hardest pilot category of all?

Because the CF-18 is the most challenging, and it's the best aircraft the Canadian forces have. It's not regular flying. Fighting the aircraft, using the weapons system and the radar makes the job challenging and difficult and that's what's kept me in this career.

What gives you your confidence?

Seeing myself improve as a fighter pilot, seeing myself get better. When people start to listen to me and respect what I have to say, then I can see that confidence reflected in me, and I think, 'Yeah, I'm getting better.'

As far as I understand, 25 per cent of a possible 500 candidates who apply to become pilots are actually chosen for pilot training. And then, of that 25 per cent, only the top people in each class are chosen to be fighter pilots, because essentially you are the elite of pilots. You're, I guess, the closest to what would be a "Top Gun." You made all the cuts. How did you do it?

By working very hard and having a lot of fun.

Fun!

Oh yes. Definitely. If I wasn't having fun, I probably wouldn't have performed as well. When I did Moose Jaw, I came third in my class and I enjoyed myself. I had a very good instructor who taught me well, and I relaxed and I did well. I'm not gonna say it wasn't difficult, it was very difficult, but it was also a pleasure doing it. Getting the top third slot just came with it, really. I knew my goal as a fighter pilot, and I knew what I had to do to get there.

So when you were training and when you were being examined, what qualities were your examiners looking for?

Obviously they were looking for basic coordination, but they were also looking for decision making skills and the ability to learn new tasks quickly. We had to go through a number of tests and emergencies, whether they were real or not. We practiced and learned to make quick and correct decisions in a fast moving aircraft. They looked for decision-making skills and they also look out for people who might become overwhelmed by the many tasks in a given situation. You must make the right decisions, and you must make them quickly.

Give me an example of an emergency situation that you're put in.

Okay, say I'm flying the CF-18 on a cross-country mission, and I lose an engine. Say I hit a bird and the bird takes out one of my engines. I would have to decide whether to return to my home base or to continue on to my destination. Factors such as fuel, weather and the possibility of a fire all must be weighed before I make my final decision. There are a number of decisions to make and timing is critical.

Is this a theoretical examination on paper, or are you actually up in the air having to do this?

You're up in the air. Although we often use the ground simulator to practice emergencies that would be too dangerous to simulate in the air. In Moose Jaw the student pilots fly a number of tests including navigation, instrument flight, aerobatics and formation flying. All of these have simulated emergencies in them.

What do you have the toughest time doing?

I would say that, at my stage, the area where I need the most work is using the CF-18 radar effectively in an air fight that has an unknown number of adversaries. I believe most fighter pilots have difficulty in this area for the pilot must not only keep track of her own wingman but must assess the adversary situation and make sound and correct tactical decisions in order to accomplish the mission and stay alive. It is something that takes a long time to develop and is quickly lost if you don't practice.

What reservations did your parents have about their daughter choosing a military flying career?

My father was enthusiastic as he wanted to be a military pilot when he first immigrated to Canada. Mom was thrilled, because I was doing what I wanted to do. They're a great support and they're very proud of me.

But don't they get nervous, I mean, you're constantly placing yourself in life-and-death situations, are you not?

What we do here in Cold Lake is essentially practice for a potential conflict. My folks understand that I love what I'm doing and that I'm safe at what I'm doing. I believe that if I was sent to a conflict and if I had the luxury of visiting home before I went, I'd have to calm their fears, and explain again that this is why I signed on to the Air Force and this is what I want to do. Certainly they would have concerns if I went into combat; the everyday flying, however, they've learned to accept.

Canada has a commitment to NATO. And you'll probably be called upon to fly and possibly fight in war zones. Have you thought about the moral implications?

No one wants a war. However, that is what I was trained to do, and if they were to send someone, I would want it to be me. If they were to send a squadron, I would want it to be my squadron, because I know how hard we train and I know how good we are. I would want us to go. I've never been in a conflict. When the Gulf War occurred, I was a student. But myself, along with every other student fighter pilot, we wished we were there to participate, because that's what we're trained to do.

The reality is that being in a war means the potential for taking other people's lives. And in order for you to protect, you may have to do that. How do you deal with that, psychologically or even morally?

Psychologically or morally. Myself I know that if Canada chose to get involved in a conflict, I am confident that we would be in a situation to protect our own troops, Canadian or NATO, and civilians. I know that Canada would never be an aggressor, we would be a protector, and that's what I believe in.

Let's forget Canada for a second. There's Kim Reid, and this other pilot in a plane is shooting at you, and in order to protect yourself you have to disable the plane and someone can lose their life, and it could be you and it could be that person. It's a big responsibility, I think, the power that you have.

It is a big responsibility and we deal with it every day in that we train for that potential situation. As a CF-18 pilot, I would fly with a wingman against any number of adversaries. Our job is to protect each other and get the mission completed. The mission may well include destroying enemy aircraft.

A wingman is someone who's flying beside you?

Yes, in another CF-18. In the heat of battle, I don't think I'd be thinking of the other person in the other aircraft. I'd be thinking about my mission. I won't be thinking about the moral of the problem, I'll be thinking about doing my job. Afterwards, yes, I probably would be. Before, I probably would be as well. During, I'd be doing my job.

And is that a discussion topic amongst the guys who you work with, the question of life and death?

I would say no, it's not a topic that we discuss at all. For good reason I believe, because when we're actually in a conflict our minds must be on the mission at hand.

Back at school, what ratio of students at your college were female?

There were 12 of us in my class, maybe a few more.

Out of how many?

Out of about 120.

Did attending military college give you enough opportunity to cultivate female friends?

Oh yes, I have some very dear friends from military college. As close as sisters if I ever had any, and I call them that.

You are Captain Kim Reid. So tell me about your rank?

I became a Captain two years ago, and that was two years after graduating from military college.

Is that fast, slow, right on schedule?

It's right on schedule. A captain holds a fair amount more responsibility than, say, a lieutenant or a second-lieutenant. As a lieutenant you probably can get away with making a few more mistakes but as a captain it is less likely. As a captain on a fighter squadron you are given organisational tasks with respect to deployment exercises and the like.

How do you avoid losing your individuality, being part of a very strong institution?

Well, I know myself, I'm a very strong individual. I have a lot of confidence. Part of that has been developed because of my being in the military. My background in the military college, in the years I spent thus far in the military, has given me a lot of self-confidence. I know who I am, I know what I want to do with my life and I don't ever feel like I'm lost in a mass of people. I am Kim Reid and this is what I do. Being the only woman fighter pilot here, people know who I am anyway. I do stick out. No, I've never had a problem with not knowing who I am or where I belong.

Let's talk about the physical demands of being at the controls of a fighter jet. I understand that the pressure when you're flying at 600 miles per hour or so, or probably faster, is a huge pressure on your body. Can you talk a bit about that?

Sure. You're right. There's a great physical demand on fighter pilots. I lift weights, and I keep fit and I have to eat well. That's a big thing. I have to make sure to eat a healthy breakfast every day, because my job is very demanding. I could hurt myself if I'm not prepared.

Okay, explain a G-force.

Well, right now you and I are sitting at one G. If I were to pull an acceleration on the body of 7.5 G in the CF-18, that's 7.5 times your weight.

Seven-and-a-half times your weight exactly, pushing against you?

Yes.

Down on you or at you?

Down, towards the centre of the earth.

This is when you're going how fast?

The faster you go, the more G you can pull in a turn. At 600 miles per hour, you'll have no problem pulling seven-and-a-half G, no problem at all.

So when you strengthen your body, how does it help you deal with the G-force?

You want to do isometric exercise that'll increase your muscle mass. You want strength. Endurance is also good, as you want to be able to keep that strength going. The idea is to get enough strength in your body to keep the blood in your brain as you're pulling a G. We also carry out a G-straining maneuver to keep the blood in the top part of your body. If your muscles are relaxed when you pull a G, it's very likely that blood could rush to your extremeties and you could black out.

It keeps the blood in your brain!?

That's right.

What's the G-strain? What is that?

A G-straining maneuver. The pilot tightens the muscles in the legs, arms and chest while pulling a G. This manoeuvre can increase your G-tolerance by up to 2-3 G. We also wear a G-suit. This suit has air bladders around the calf, thigh, and abdomen muscles which inflate and squeeze if you pull more than 2 G. It also adds about 2 extra G to your G-tolerance.

Tell me what that is like.

Well, I wasn't initially prepared for G when flying the Tutor in Moose Jaw. I learned how to cope with it and eventually it wasn't a problem. Some pilots say they enjoy it, but I can't admit to that. When I'm fighting my jet, however, there's a lot of adrenaline and I don't realize that I'm pulling G until afterwards when I glance at the G-meter and say, "Wow, that was 7 G." I don't really notice it much anymore unless I missed breakfast or haven't flown an aggressive mission in a while.

There have been stories of fellow pilots blacking out.

Yes, that's why we developed the G-straining maneuver and the G-suit. The new generation of aircrafts are capable of pulling more G than the pilots are. The limiting factor is the pilot.

I was talking to Manon Rhéaume, the first professional female goalie. She says that she has always had to be tougher than the guys. For example, whenever she has injuries, she very rarely reports them until she either blacks out or until her arm is hanging by a thread. I mean, she puts herself in the line of fire, big time. Because she knows that those guys, and the media and the critics, in her case, are always looking for the slightest sign of weakness in her. Is this your experience as well?

I'd have to say it's not. Perhaps because I know that if I let an injury go too far, my career could be over. If I hurt my back and I didn't go to the medical officer, it would just get worse and there would be a point where I could not fly again. As a student—and most pilots would say this—you feel pressured to just keep on flying, but as an older, wiser fighter pilot I won't fly if I'm sick. It's dangerous and I could get myself killed if I'm not careful. That's the bottom line. Most of us are very smart that way. We will pull ourselves off the flying program if we are sick.

Is there any teasing happening?

Oh, yeah. All the time.

Do you get teased more than the guys, or how are you treated? And tell me the truth.

I am going to tell you the truth. I get teased a lot. But as soon as they stop teasing, that's when I'll be worried. Their teasing me lets me know that I belong. They feel comfortable in teasing me. And when I say teasing, I don't mean anyone being nasty or rude or trying to get a reaction—I mean good fun.

I've heard stories of locker talk, which is perfectly natural. I mean, you get a bunch of guys together and—watch out. Now you're considered one of the guys, does your locker talk match theirs?

My locker talk—I firmly believe that I will not change who I am to try to fit in with the boys. They accept Kim for who Kim is. I don't swear unless I'm mad. I don't smoke cigars. That's not who I am and that's not what I'd be to try to fit in. Sometimes they will curb their language or they'll apologize to me if they don't know me. They can choose to talk around me like that or choose not to. I've never asked them to behave in a certain way around me. And I've never tried to match them curse for curse either. That's not who I am.

Can you describe a typical day at the base?

Well, I can describe today for you, if you like. I woke up at 6:00 a.m., I got to work at seven o'clock. I read until our squadron operation brief at 7:30. We finished our operations brief at eight o'clock.

And what is the operations brief?

Well, it's where we got our meteorology, and...

So that would be the weather.

Yes, the weather. Then our air maintanance officer briefed the squadron on the serviceability of our jets. We adjusted the flying schedule accordingly and also received an intelligence briefing. Our intelligence section on squadron is responsible for keeping the pilots up to speed with respect to world events and for training us in aircraft recognition. Afterwards, I had a meeting at Wing Operations with repect to an up and coming squadron deployment to Inuvik, NWT. We will be deploying 6 jets to our Forward Operation Location, FOL, in order to participate in a joint Canada–USA NORAD exercise. I spent an hour and a half discussing the logistics of this operation. I came back to the squadron and went into a mission brief. It was a sweep mission. I lead 2 CF-18s on a mission to protect 2 bombers. Two T-33s simulated two Soviet Su-25 bombers. We went against two adversary CF-18s who were trying to shoot down the bombers before they reached their target and to shoot us down. The mission lasted about one hour and fifteen minutes and we spent one hour and a half debriefing the mission. After, I went to the gym to play some volleyball and lift some weights. I got home about fifteen minutes before you called.

Holy smokes!

You do a fair amount of physical training.

What kind of mental training do you do to keep yourself in top form?

Well, I keep myself informed by reading *Newsweek*, *Maclean's* and *Time*. My squadron is the contingency fighter squadron for the Canadian Armed Forces, which means that if we were asked to go to an area of conflict, my squadron would be chosen. It's my responsibility to be up on world events. I also take correspondence courses with the University of Waterloo. I'm taking a break this semester, however, because I found it difficult to do my job effectively and study for these courses.

What sort of courses were you taking?

I was taking organic chemistry and molecular biology.

Wow.

Well, I have other goals, other dreams. I would like to be involved in space sciences some day. Ten years from now I might want to persue a medical degree. Right now I'm taking courses that will make this transition easier.

Let's go back to your in-the-air-training. When you do these maneuvers, obviously they're choreographed, but someone could black out. I understand the smallest mistake can be fatal. Have you ever had any close calls?

Oh yes. I don't think there's a fighter pilot who hasn't had a close call. Sure, there are close calls. You're moving very quickly and fighting multiple adversaries who are probably all travelling to the same point in the sky. We have what we call a "big sky theory" which suggests that space and the odds are in your favour. However, planes look small in that big sky and things happen fast.

Describe your close call.

Well, I'll describe one. I was in Miramar, California with my squadron and I was fighting against an A6. Now, compared to a CF-18, the A6s is a very, very tiny aircraft. I turned towards this fellow and he came up underneath me. I couldn't see his canopy, so I knew he could not see me. So I just turned for all it was worth. I don't know how close we came, but he never saw me, and I just saw him at the last second. My heart was just a thumpin' afterwards as we came very close to hitting. That's probably the closest I've ever come. I would not say it is a common occurrence. Whenever it happens, we come down and talk about it. We discuss why a "near miss" happened and try to learn the lesson that will prevent it from happening again. In this case the other pilot didn't have enough situational awareness prior to coming to the merge.

Meaning he didn't know what was going on around him?

Not well enough to be able to access the situation quicker than what he did. Mistakes happen, and sometimes you're not up to full form—you take that as a lesson. Next time, you make sure it doesn't happen.

You obviously have a high tolerance in the fear category. What pushes your fear button?

I have to say that becoming lackadaisical or over-confident, that's my biggest fear. The CF-18 is a wonderful machine. It has a lot of magic in it and it's easy to fly. It's user-friendly. The controls and the computers all make your tasks easy and quick, and you can get very good at manipulating the controls and systems of your aircraft. But if you let your guard down and if you don't keep your mind sharp, then a mistake can easily happen because of the extreme task loading of the missions that we do. You can end up hitting the ground or hitting another aircraft. I'm scared of losing that sharp edge or not being in full form.

So, like I said before, if I'm feeling ill, I won't fly, because I know I'm not sharp enough.

Yours is a contingency squadron, which means you may be seeing action this year. What about the realization or the reality that, instead of maybe being on the winning side, you're on the losing side and you're captured. What kind of preparation do you make for those kinds of occurrences?

How can you prepare for something like that?

I don't know, you tell me, Kim.

I don't even know. Honestly, I don't know how you'd prepare for something like that. I have a number of friends in the States who were involved in the Gulf War and had friends who were captured. It was a devastating experience for them. I never talked to an individual who was actually captured. I can't imagine being absolutely prepared for such a situation. Getting captured by people with different customs, religious beliefs and possibly less respect for life or human rights than you or I have is a scary proposition. It's not something that I dwell on. It is definitely not something that I dwell on.

Is it something that your superiors bring up? Are you educated about the possibilities?

If my squadron was chosen to go to a conflict, we would be educated. All those that went to the Gulf War were given several briefings. But this is not something that we want on our minds when we are flying. If we were actually going into a conflict, we would discuss the possiblity of capture but we would not dwell on it. The main job is clear—to fly the aircraft and do your job.

What about the fun stuff? You are on a base with a lot of very handsome men. Can you date these guys? Or does that interfere with your working relationship?

I've had several discussions about that with my previous commanding officer. He said it wasn't a problem if I wanted to date one of the fellas on squadron. It's my life, and I can choose. I learned very early on in my career, however, that your work is work and your private life is private. When I go to work, I recognize the men as colleagues. I couldn't go out and fight with them, and then go out for dinner that night as an intimate couple. I could not see myself doing that. It's very clear to me that they are working colleagues and that's all. I understand the dangers of getting involved with someone you work with. If things didn't work out, then you still have to fly and work with this person. That could put a lot of strain on you, the other person and probably on your squadron as well. The squadron has to come first. So I would never do anything to harm the squadron or to put any strain on anybody, anybody in the squadron.

You're all so dependent on each other, you're a team.

Yes, it has to be a professional relationship, and I think the guys appreciate my attitude.

Someone at the base describes you in the following way: 'She's very beautiful. When she's suited up, she looks every bit the part of a fighter pilot, and when she's dressed up in her high heels, you'd never believe that she is a fighter pilot.'

So who said that?

I'm not allowed to tell. How do guys react when you put your high heels on and they see the sexy side?

I believe they think it's great, because they recognize that Kim is being Kim, and Kim is a woman and Kim is a fighter pilot, you don't have to differentiate between the two. They respect that and appreciate it. They would respect me less if I tried to act like one of the guys.

It must be tough for you to think about settling down. I mean, if you wanted to start a family, for example, you would have to stop flying for at least part of that time.

At this stage in my life, I'm doing exactly what I love to do. I would not consider having a family because my job is 10-12 hours a day. I haven't really met anyone to compete with flying the CF-18.

That may happen in the future, and in fact some day, I hope it does because I'd love to have someone to grow old with. That would be wonderful. But for now, I'm in love with my jet.

What are the disadvantages of being a fighter pilot?

Oh, well, the long days, it's very competitive in the fighter pilot world. I'm not sure if that's a disadvantage or not, but you have to work hard if you want to be good.

What are the advantages?

Oh, the flying, the incredible job that I do. The people I work with are incredibly intelligent. People say, 'Kim, it must be tough working with a bunch of guys.' Well, no it's not, they're very open-minded and they all have a great sense of humor. I'm in my niche, so I'm happy where I am.

I think the fact that you're doing this proves that women can be and are effective fighter pilots. So I ask you, Kim Reid, why do you think there aren't more women doing what you're doing?

Oh! I've asked myself that so many times. It could be a number of reasons. It could be fear, there is certainly an aura around the fighter pilot community of what we're supposedly like. As you probably know, a stereotype is rarely what defines a group. There's a fear that it's cut-throat, that there's lots of backstabbing and people are nasty in the fighter world. Well, no, that's not the case. There's a lot of teasing, but everybody's teased. I'm not sure if that would disuade women. It may be also an economic problem, we're not hiring as many people any more, unless you already have previous flying training or are with the military college program. I believe it is much more difficult to become a pilot with the Canadian Armed Forces. Our southern neighbors, however, just graduated 15 pilots.

These are all women?

These are all women, yes. The United States have a larger population to draw from. Historically, women pilots have always been a small minority in the military of both countries. I honestly believe time will change that. However, like I said before, the teenage girls that I meet with eyes as big as saucers keep my hope and conviction strong. When they say, 'Boy, I really want to do what you're doing.' Well, I hope that sticks with them right into their 20s and they actually go for it.

What's the best advice you've ever been given from anyone that helps you get through the rough times?

Don't give up. Never give up.

Who told you that?

It was a man named Pat Howell. He's presently a fighter pilot with 419 Squadron here in Cold Lake. I met him in Baden, Germany when he was a young fighter pilot on 409 Squadron. I had a few months before my fighter-pilot training started. I had gone over to Germany to find out what a real fighter squadron was like. Many of the pilots were looking at me from the side saying, 'Who is this woman? I wonder what she's going to be like?' And I sat talking with Pat one Friday evening at the officer's bar and he said, 'Kim, never give up. The last two women did and, in the eyes of the guys, they wished they hadn't.' He said, 'Why didn't they just stick it through and prove themselves? Even though you make mistakes and you screw up, so what—don't give up.' That was the best advice I've ever had.

We're going to end with a very serious question here, Kim. Flying demands a mental and physical discipline. It doesn't lend itself to rash, impulsive actions. So what do you do when you pass a store window and there's a gorgeous dress priced way beyond your budget? Do you exercise control? Or do you go for it anyway?

If I really loved it?

Yeah.

Oh, I'd buy it.

You mean, you would act rash?

Oh, yes, it's a dress. Definitely. No lives are at stake, just my pocketbook.

Kingi Carpenter

Kingi Carpenter is a well-known face around Toronto's trendy Queen Street area. With her tousled blonde hair, very pink lipsticked lips and retro sling-back pumps, she looks the part of a wacky gal who just wants to have fun.

In this case, appearances are somewhat deceiving. It's true that Kingi is having the time of her life, but it's sheer determination, a unique vision and a good marketing sense that have established her as a force to be reckoned with in the fashion scene. What originally attracted me to Kingi was her innovative approach to designing clothes. After spending two hours in her store, I was just as interested in her thoughts on how to run a business. Kingi is an eccentric entrepreneur.

I first met Kingi almost seven years ago when she was beginning her career in fashion. She was using the Ontario College of Art silk-screen studio to experiment with wild fabric patterns. After a few years of sewing lessons, she turned her silk-screened fabrics into a collection of streetwear she named Peach Berserk in honor of her favorite nail-polish shade. The colors she works with also have groovy names like Ape Red and Pompous Purple. Her print designs are inspired by pop culture of the '50s, '60s and '70s, especially the cosmetics, cookbooks and Harlequin romances of the time. Between the Kool-aid colors and kitschy concepts, the final look is pretty out there. Because she played by her own rules, it's taken years for the mainstream design community to catch up with her and take her seriously.

Today Kingi Carpenter is sitting pretty in her brand-new downtown Toronto storefront location. In keeping with that wacky persona of hers, the walls of her store are pink and covered with girlish photos from the last few decades and the racks are a rainbow of outrageous outfits. It's studied chaos, resembling a teenage girl's messy bedroom. Meanwhile, the back half of the space is quite practical, filled with the equipment necessary to cut, sew and screen her whole collection. A large scrapbook sits by the cash register illustrating the possibilities of using Peach Berserk silk-screened fabric to reupholster your furniture. And just beside this handmade catalogue lies a stack of six-page Peach Berserk newsletters for customers and the media. At this point it becomes very clear that Kingi has set up a solid, well-thought-out business venture.

Kingi is always animated when she talks about her zany streetwear, which she smilingly explains was inspired by her favorite book, *Sex and the Single Girl*. When the focus of our conversation eventually shifted to the business end of her work, a more serious Kingi emerged. I watched her become more intense as she explained her views on business management. Just as she has succeeded in the design world by doing what she feels is right, she's applying the same principles to the business side of her life. Kingi is an innovative entrepreneur who understands the economic climate of the '90s. And she's having fun doing it.

You've been described as 'the self-professed queen of the hair-dye bottles,' 'undressed without lipstick'—not a pair of flat shoes to your name, as the Bette Midler of fashion design. But who do you see?

I think a lot of that's true. I cultivate that image. Because I feel more myself if I'm wearing high heels and lipstick. I don't try to fight it. It's fun for me. I like it and so that's what I do and I don't try to pretend to be anything else. It's my form of feminism. This is what I like, this is what I've chosen and I'm going to flaunt it. So they're pretty accurate. Except I don't think I look like Bette Midler.

No, I think it's more that you may be as flamboyant as her. So what's the look that you're going for here in your new store?

Fun, and very pink. The opposite of fashion stores that try to be very chic, everything straight and orderly and neat. We're messy and we like our pink walls and we like our crazy floor and we have an excuse for being like this because we make our things. So we have cut pieces of fabric around and scissors lying around everywhere. It's a less serious way of looking at fashion. I think it gets into the store as much as our clothes and our attitudes.

You grew up on a farm. But looking at this very groovy place, one wouldn't think it.

My parents wanted to live on a farm. It was that kind of late '60s thing to move to the country, get back to nature, have more space and have a place where your children could run around more, be more themselves. Running around on the farm and not wearing any clothes. So I think the fact that I had parents like that has helped me be the way I am. They weren't very conventional. We weren't regular farmers. Although we did farm.

What did you grow?

We grew corn. We sold a lot—300 dozen a day on a good day.

Three hundred dozen!?

Yeah—on the side of the road.

Did you have to do a lot of work in the fields?

I didn't because I'm really allergic to things, so I was the salesperson. I would sit on the side of the road and sell the corn, in my bathing suit. That was really fun for me, because I liked the sales aspect. Sometimes when I see a car slow down outside my store, even now, I remember the thrill of a car stopping to buy corn. And it was so much fun selling it. Me and my brother and sister would think of crazy ways of making them buy more corn. We made signs and we had a crazy little table. That was mostly my job, while my brother and sister were picking the corn with my parents. And then my father had this attitude, because he was very socialist, that everybody got paid equally. So at the end of the day everybody got the same amount of money for doing the corn. We also had cows. We had up to 60 beef cows and six different gardens on the farm, because my father was really into growing all our own vegetables. He was really into being self-sufficient and producing all our own things. He was very frugal that way.

How is it, when I look at you, I can't imagine you growing up on a farm?

I don't know, because I really liked it. In fact I took a whole year off school and stayed home on the farm. When I was 14, me and my dad planted everything ourselves and I was so into it—if I saw a weed, I would freak out. We even had a maple-syrup industry. We had university students come and tap trees for us and we would help them. So we had some really groovy hippies out doing our maple syrup. And then my sister would get crushes on them. It was totally fun.

My father was a general in the air force, so we moved to the farm when he retired. And then I went away to school, because my father had gone to a private school. My sister and I both went to Havergal and my brother went to Upper Canada College for a few months before he got kicked out. I think coming to Toronto was a good thing for me. It was a whole different world. I had fun.

Were you very close to your Dad?

I think he has a lot to do with the way I am, actually.

In what way?

Well, we talked a lot. We spent a lot of time together. He made me feel I could do anything I wanted to do. I carry that with me all the time. He had a sense of humor about everything. I saw him do whatever he wanted and not even flinch. I'd sometimes feel he was embarrassing me. But he'd just say whatever he felt. And he would dress in his own way. He was really messy. He always wore these red shorts. Very old-fashioned shorts, like trousers, because he was very old-fashioned in his own crazy way, and they were always red, and I thought that was so nice. His hair grew straight up and he wouldn't cut it, he'd forget. I remember talking to my father—I'd talk to him when he'd be in the tub—those were our best talks. And he said something like—I could do whatever I wanted. He said, 'Kingi, this really sounds silly, but you could be Prime Minister if you wanted to.' Not that that's anything I'd ever want to do, but it struck me because I really listened to anything he had to say and I thought, 'Oh, my father thinks I can do anything.' And I've never forgotten that moment. I just admired him. He was so smart and he cared about people so much. I think people give generals a bad name.

Well, there's a stereotype that goes with it. Like the one I had of the private school.

School was good for me, because when I was 15, my father died, and after my father died our family disintegrated a bit. So my brother Fred went away to school, my sister was in university and I think it was good for me to be away from the farm. I had a best friend that I met as soon as school started—she's still my best friend. So that was good and we hung out together and the other girls thought we were crazy. It wouldn't have been the same without her.

The picture I have of private school is of uniforms and being conservative and fitting in. You seem to do your own thing.

I don't think there's any more fitting in than there is in any other school and I also feel that the uniform—you can have more individuality when you have a uniform, because there's more subtle things you can do to make your uniform different. You don't have to worry so much about your clothes being in style because you're forced to wear this ugly uniform, so no one can say, 'Why are you wearing that?' And little things, like doing up your hem with tape or having your kilt cut in slits in every one of the pleats. See, I just cut a slit in every pleat and for some reason, I didn't get in trouble for that. But you got in trouble if your hem was down, or if your socks were down you got in big trouble. My friend had a pen that said 'Homework causes brain damage' and she got in terrible trouble. Really bad trouble. They were so weird at Havergal. You saw the little ironies or stupidity there, because there were so many rules. It's so institutionalized and so traditional that you really see all the stupid things they do. We just laughed at them because it was so strict. But we really had fun. There were no guys around so there was no one to impress, we had a really good time. I think it was a whole lot better for me than living at home.

That's why it was good to go to Havergal, I think. To see that side of the world. I think it's good that I went to university, because if I hadn't gone, I'd have thought, 'Oh, people who've gone to university are so smart. And they learn such good things. And the work is so difficult in university, I never could have done it.' And now I know it wasn't that hard and people weren't that smart—they were regular people.

Speaking of university, you did a couple of years at McGill in Montreal where you studied political science. When did you start designing?

I studied political science because—I guess it's partly to do with thinking you have to take a certain route in life. When I finished Havergal, I thought, 'You have to go to university, have to be educated.' So I studied political science because I've always had an interest in it. But I realized when I was there that I wasn't the type to sit in a lecture for three hours or go to the library and do tons of reading. I always liked to make my own clothes, and I also liked to draw and make things. But it never occurred to me that you can study something you like to do, drawing and making things, and actually have a job with that. Your job is something serious, you know. So I think that's when I actually grew up and matured—halfway through my second year, I went to the university office to drop out, without telling anyone. It just occurred to me—I thought, 'I don't have to do this. It's just as good if I go to art school and figure out what I want to do there, than be here, not really doing that well.' So I went and the registrar said, 'Good luck to you, and I hope you're going to be okay.' That was a really important move in my life.

So you dropped out and you left Montreal?

I stayed for the rest of the year and got a job as a waitress, even though I didn't speak any French, and left in April.

You came back to Toronto?

Yes.

And you were how old at this point?

I suppose I was 20.

And what did you do when you came back to Toronto?

I worked at Simpsons—the doll department.

The doll department?

Yes. I worked a lot of places, because I didn't last too long at any of my jobs—but that's good. I've quite a good job education. I would do anything. It was too late to apply to OCA at that point, so I went to night school and took three classes at night, thinking, 'Look, Kingi, you've got to do something serious. You've got to take three classes and start to get back together.' And then I just worked at whatever job that would have me.

Why did you choose the Ontario College of Art?

It was an art school in Toronto and it was downtown, and I figured it would be good to learn something practical. Because one thing about Havergal was they didn't have any really practical art education. I never learned what a silk-screen was, or a camera, for example.

So OCA was good in the sense that I took courses in every single field. In the second year, when I was 22 years old, I took silk-screening and I loved it. I also took a course in fabric design, mostly because I had the feeling I wanted to make a dress for myself with an Eiffel Tower on it. I thought that would be something really fun to do. I had all these schemes of how I could do it and they were all totally crazy—they were nuts. So I took the course and I learned how the silk-screens worked and I printed this thing and I totally loved it, it was such fun. My first print. I picked up the silk-screen—I totally remember the moment—I picked it up—'Wow that's so neat, so great,' and I showed it to friends, and from then on you couldn't get me out of the studio—I lived in there.

That's when you decided to go into fashion design.

Yes. I figured if I did the prints, I had to do the clothes to go with them.

But your teachers told you not to. Why did they try to persuade you to stay away from that field?

Partly they thought that the types of designs I was doing wouldn't sell and I couldn't get a job. Secondly, I was too nutsy. And I didn't put my projects together properly. Basically, they looked at me and thought, 'This just isn't going to work.' But I made my silk-screens—I knew what I wanted.

Usually students respect their teachers to a certain degree, assuming they have a certain amount of knowledge. Yet something made you keep on going despite their discouragement.

Well, I've never totally respected the opinion of a teacher, they're just teachers. I think that's something I learned from my father. Just because someone has a job doesn't mean they're qualified. So I didn't take them very seriously, because I knew what I wanted to do. And once I got the idea, nobody could stop me. In fact, it made me want to do it more, to show them that they were wrong. I didn't even get accepted into OCA when I first applied. I wasn't even put on a waiting list. Everybody I knew was put on a waiting list or got accepted. I was the only person who got a letter saying, 'We don't want you at all.'

Then how did you get in?

I got into one of these moods and went marching down to the school and talked to the registrar and said, 'Look, I want to know why I'm not accepted here.' I wasn't going to let them decide my fate because, had they not accepted me and if I'd listened to them, I would never have learned silk-screening. It might have taken me a whole other year to get in. So I had an appeal interview. And probably anybody that appeals gets in.

It shows that you really wanted to be there.

That was another reason I tried really hard. Because they didn't accept me. I had to prove they were wrong.

You wanted the practical experience for silk-screening?

Yes. And they had all the equipment, all the chemicals. It gave you all that free time to do the work you wanted to do. You just had to put up with them judging your work once every term.

When I first met you, years ago, the first thing you did was hand me a copy of the book *Sex and the Single Girl* by Helen Gurley Brown. What is your fascination with her?

I found it when I was 18, in a used-clothing store. I used to love going into used-clothing stores. And the book really did influence my life. She talked about your career and the fun your career could be and how you should make it a fun thing and it should be really important in your life, and all the fun you could have being single for a while when you're an adult. And choosing your own path in life and making things fun. But it really influenced me. I read the book for years. I took it everywhere I went. And I've read all the sequels. I think Helen has really influenced the way I run this business and the way I lived through my 20s especially.

How does she affect the way you run the business?

I guess just doing it my own way and working really hard at it—I guess it comes down to the harder you work at your job, the more fun you get out of it in the end. Not to think of your job as just a way of making money, but think of it as a means to having fun. And yes, if you do a good job at it, you'll make some money. But it should be more than that and you will derive all the other things from life other than money. It will really become your social life and you'll meet interesting people if you have an interesting job and you'll learn a lot of things and you'll travel and you'll have adventures if you go about your job properly. I couldn't wait to get out there and get my own apartment and do all those things.

So she celebrates being a woman.

Yes she does.

Is that feminism?

Well it is to me. I think of feminism as being a choice and doing what you want. Thinking of what you want and doing it, whatever that might be. That's her feminism, because it's what she wants to do and she's done what she's wanted and had fun and had a really interesting time doing exactly what she wanted. And that's what I do. I figured out what I wanted and I didn't care what anyone thought. What else can feminism be?

How do you define beauty?

I know what I find beautiful, but I don't know what everybody else does. There's a sort of sensibility that I like, from different eras—from the '50s era and very Parisian-looking, *joie de vivre* images. Things that are very happy and fun. And that's what I do with my work. I try to incorporate that into the clothes I make. I like things with a sense of humor and things that are very feminine. For me, that's very beautiful.

Have you had any surprising reactions to your clothes?

Oh yes, sure. There have been people who've said to me, 'Oh, you shouldn't put images of irons on dresses, because it's so anti-feminism.' But there seem to be some people who understand them and then other people who don't. But that's fine. I think it's better to do clothes that people either love or hate rather than something mediocre.

Our generation is living in a time where boundaries have been broken down for women. Our parents had to fight, or our mothers had to fight, and say, 'I'm not going to iron that, dear, iron it yourself.' They had to break the rules. So feminism was a really big issue even one generation back. Today, feminism is equality. We seem to take it for granted.

I don't think I take it for granted. There's a difference now. It used to be harder for women. I think it was harder for them and harder for women 20 years before them and 20 years before them. I think it's gotten better. I think there are certain problems now that didn't exist then, too.

Like what?

I think that women, in some ways, are expected to do so much more, because you have so much more choice. There are so many more options open to you. Even with scientific changes in the world—reproductive technology and types of plastic surgery. These things exist and women are supposed to use them, which I think is really difficult. But I think that just having a job and going out in the world is easier for us, so we can look at it with a bit more of a light-hearted point of view.

When people walk in your store and they need to find someone to pay, do they go to your boyfriend or to you?

People tend to treat us equally when we're in here, because this is my place. When you're in somebody's house, you treat them with respect. But I find that often when I phone suppliers, they still treat a female voice differently than they treat a male voice. So there are times when I'll ask my boyfriend to do that, just because it's easier. He's not called 'honey' on the phone as often as I am. Like, if you're ordering lumber or something. I think they treat a man better.

How do you fit into the world of fashion?

I started my business at a really lucky time. The late '80s was a time when fashion began to fragment and everything was in style. Long dresses, short dresses—any color was in style and I like that, because it means that you can have your own little business and do whatever you like, no matter what is supposedly 'in fashion.' You have your own little niche. Stick to your guns and do the styles you like. I think that is integrity in a business—that you do what you like. There's a difference between businesses that do what they think will sell and businesses that do what they like. I think it makes a huge difference.

What's your favorite outfit that you designed?

That's funny, because you would think there would be one thing that really stood out and I don't think that there is. My pillowcase dresses? I really liked my pillowcase dresses, but then I liked other dresses.

What's a pillowcase dress?

It's a very momentous thing, my pillowcase dress, because it was the first idea I had for a dress. It was when I was at McGill. I could never find clothes I liked because in the early '80s, there weren't a lot of cool things around. I stayed over at my friend's place and I was sleeping in her bed and I woke up. I looked at her pillowcase and it was pink striped. It was an old pillowcase from the '60s that she'd got from her parents' house. It was these really beautiful pink and white stripes, cotton. I looked at it and I said, 'Suzy, can I have your pillowcase?' And she said, 'Okay, if you give me yours.' So I gave her my pillowcase and I slept with her pillowcase for the rest of the year. What I did is I took it and I sewed it into a T-shirt. I cut the T-shirt off and made straps. It looked really nice. I put on a shiny, black hipster belt and I wore it until it was in shreds. I still have pictures of it. Then I made all these other pillowcase dresses and then I started wearing pillowcases—they just had a head hole and armholes in them. There were all these rumors going around that I was wearing bed sheets. I guess those dresses were important to me. I'll always remember my pillowcase era.

Legend has it that your company name—Peach Berserk—comes from a nail-polish color. The colors you use, even the wild names of your dresses, are all really wacky. But I find that when I talk to you, you're far less wacky than one might

expect. I wonder if you have what I would almost describe as a stage persona.

I think that I'm really quite a logical person. But it's like this fantasy world that I create with what I do, which is fun for me. It all comes together with what I do. The prints, and the names of the prints, and the colors I use and the styles I use, they all have names. Because they all become their own little world and it's a world I can go into whenever I want to. So there's the color Tiptoe Through the Turquoise, Cheese Me Cheesies is a print and there's the Madeline dress. It's a whole world. I think when people see me or see my place, they expect me to be just silly and not so sensible. Sometimes in my life I've thought it was good to be able to hide your true self at times and not let everybody know what you're really like. When I was younger, I was like that. People would say, 'Doesn't it bug you that everyone thinks you're stupid, Kingi?' and I would say, 'Well, if they think I'm stupid, then they're the ones who aren't very perceptive. Let them think that. If they just look at me, at the way I look, and think I'm stupid, then they aren't being very smart.' Because other people knew what I was like. But it's good to be able to go in and out of the Peach Berserk world. It can't be your whole life, you know. We don't put any Peach Berserk prints upstairs in our apartment. Unless we run out of fabric and have nothing else to use, because you've got to get away from it sometimes.

Does it work to your benefit that people perceive you as wacky, whimsical and very feminine, whereas underneath it all there's a cunning businesswoman?

Probably. It's more fun for people to think of me as wacky. Instead of thinking, 'She's an intelligent businesswoman.' That's kind of boring. That's not as much fun at a party. It's good for people to think of me as a crazy party girl. Who would you rather take out for dinner? So sure. It's like acting. A job like this includes a bit of theatrics and I'll play that up. And if people want to see the other side of me, then I'll talk about that, too.

To me, you're living proof that you don't have to necessarily fit in to be successful.

I think you're more successful if you don't fit in. I think being a misfit's good. If you're a misfit, you're forced to use your cunning to survive. I was in that position when I started my business. Because I was, like, 'Okay, my mother doesn't speak to me, so that's cut off, I don't have any money, I don't have an education'—because I didn't graduate from OCA either, got fired from every job—13 in a row. I thought, 'Kingi, what are you going to do with yourself? You can be a waitress for the rest of your life and keep getting fired'—because I never got along with the managers of restaurants. So I thought, 'Okay, you've got to make it yourself.' And also I'd found what I liked to do, so those things converged. I thought, 'You've got to work hard.' And every time I didn't want to get up in the morning, I'd just say to myself, 'Do you want to go back to Mother's Pizza? No. I don't.' So I really think that misfits are better off.

I agree. I'm one. What's your definition of success?

Success is being happy and enjoying what you do. Because your time is really the most important thing in your life that you have and that you spend it in a happy, fulfilling way. Not how much money you make, or how much power and fame in the world you have. Just getting up in the morning and enjoying what you do. I'll be working on something and then I'll think, 'I'm going to cut out some jackets this afternoon—okay, that's going to be really fun.'

Look at the smile on your face!

Yeah, because I enjoy it. Then I'll think, 'I want to work on that new print.' I'll get that new print down and it's going to be the best one I've done. To me, that's really fun. It's enjoying yourself and waking up and liking to go to work. Being excited about your job. Enjoying your work and not just looking forward to the weekend or going on a vacation, because if that's what you're doing, you're wasting your time. I know people who do that, who are totally wasting their time. And no money, I think, is worth that.

Alison Reid

"I'm not defying death, I'm outsmarting it."

(The National Ballet of Canada)

Jennifer Fournier

"I don't see someone dance, I see the dance..."

(Master Corporal Fitzpatrick)

Kim Reid

"At this stage in my life, I would not consider having a family...for now, I'm in love with my jet."

(Chris Chapman)

Kingi Carpenter

"I think you're more successful if you don't fit in. If you're a misfit, you're forced to use your cunning to survive."

(Michal Boland)

Ann Duggan

"If I decide that I want to do something, I think about how I can accomplish my goal and then I work for it."

(Photo and Imaging: Yanka and Yolanda Van Der Kolk, Twenty-One)

Sarah Polley

"No one's ever put limitations on me. That's how I'd want to influence people, to let them know there are no bars too strong to break."

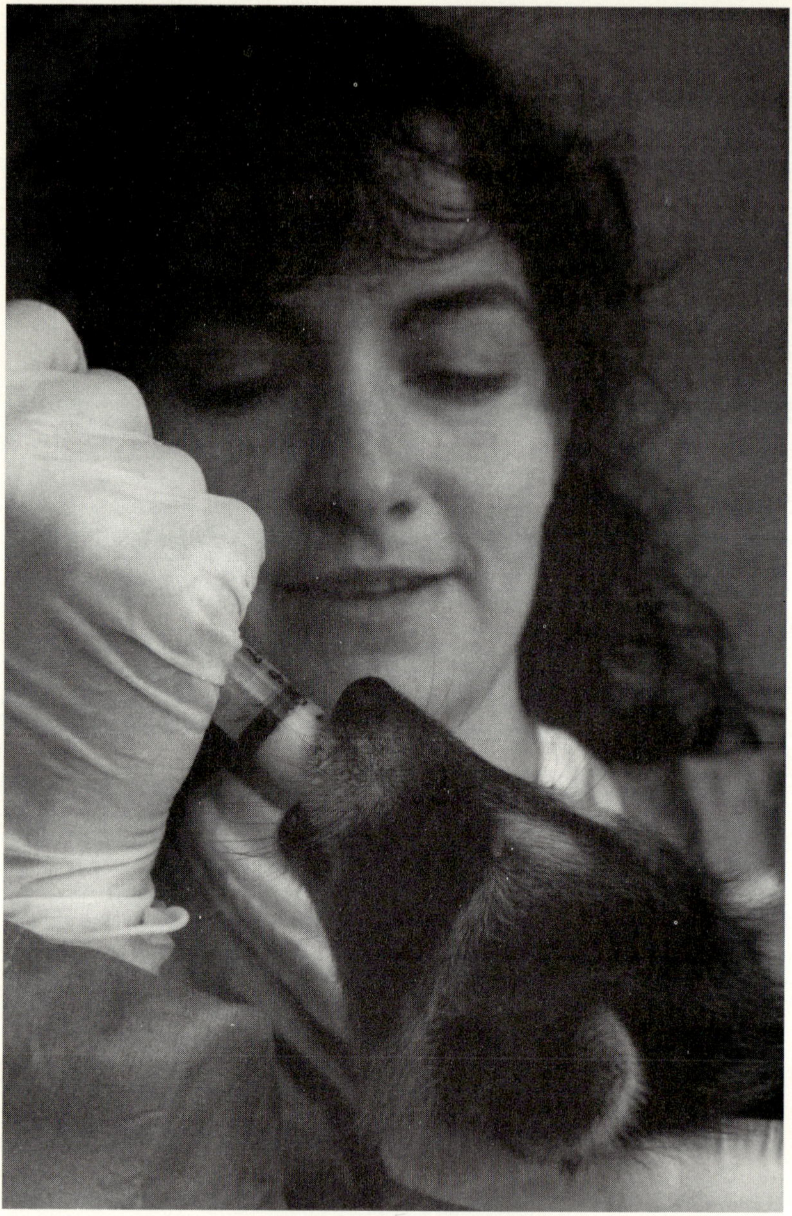

(The Toronto Star)

Nathalie Karvonen

"Unless an animal has been affected by a person, I know what to expect. People aren't like that. You never know what to expect from a person on the street."

(George Whiteside)

Susan Aglukark

"A lot of my decision-making is based on the 35,000 people I represent. So my window, or view, is based on that vast part of Canada that nobody ever really thinks about—people that are Inuit."

Severn Cullis-Suzuki

"What I hope all Canadians will do—I think this is one of the biggest steps we have to take—is to look around and not take so much for granted."

(Karen Hill)

Sarah McLachlan

"I don't mind people looking up to me, because I believe in what I'm doing and therefore it's okay for other people to believe in me.

For the past 12 years, I've seen many young designers come and go, but I rarely see them move to a bigger place, which you've just done. So what do you think it is that you're doing that allows you to be this successful?

I have a lot of perseverance. I work a lot and I stick to my main ideal of what I want to do with my business.

Which is?

I keep wanting to improve, to build on it and make it better. I want to add to the print collection I have and the styles that I make. I also don't spend money where I don't have to. I think a lot of people decide they're going to be designers and then go blow a lot of money. I never had a lot of money. When you first met me, I had just started the business on nothing, out of the apartment. Since I've never had money to lose, I could never go bankrupt. I couldn't afford to. It's really true. No one would lend me money. I couldn't get any credit anywhere. A lot of people spend money and go get themselves something like a fax machine when you don't have to have a fax machine. I've seen it happen. I've seen the whole thing come and go with people starting businesses, and I think that you can be really creative on no money and these days people really appreciate that. They think that the cleverness it takes to make things interesting with no money is more appealing than a business that has tons of money. I think it's a modern way of doing business. It's cultivated doing things inexpensively. We have people who work for us on a trade system. We teach them how to print and teach them everything we know, and in exchange they work for us. They sew on buttons and they print for us. Ever since I've started, I've had people work that way. And I can't get rid of them. They come to me. I build up these really good friendships. And you tend to get the most interesting people that way. The people who don't get paid work better than the people who do. That's rule number one. It's because they want to learn and they're not here to punch a clock. We respect them for what they're doing and we try and make sure it's fair, that they learn. That's one way that you save money and also build a good relationship. It builds a nice spirit in the store.

I think there's a certain way to treat people who work for you. Because I can't pay people very well, I say, 'Look, I can't pay you very well, but you can make your own silk-screen and print it here. I'll treat you really nicely.' I've been treated so horribly by bosses when I was working in restaurants. The way that you never let other people treat you, but you'll put up with from the manager of a restaurant. And I thought, 'I'm not going to be that way with people.'

When I came here, I came to interview a designer. I see you now as an entrepreneur.

I don't know which one I think of myself as. In terms of being an entrepreneur, I suppose that's a risk-taker, because I like taking risks. I love going in and buying fabric, even if I don't have a lot of money. Over the years I've thought to myself, 'Look, you can keep this money or you can buy fabric, and if I sell it, I'll have five times as much.'

When things weren't going well, when you didn't have a business partner and things were a lot harder, what got you through the tough times?

For me, it's always been tough times because when I started—it wasn't quite the recession yet, but I was just starting out and no one had heard of me or took me seriously. I expected it to be tough. Maybe that's what's wrong with me. Because I'm lucky enough to be doing my own thing, get up in the morning when I choose, run my business the way I choose, I do my own artwork all day, I run things the way I want, I'm there when I want, so I expect it to be tough because that's a good trade-off. Because I think it's a fair trade-off and I'm constantly building up what I do, even though it doesn't pay off monetarily yet, I'm building it up, I'm behind the scenes.

I'm building up my print collection and my clothing collection and I'm slowly getting better known, so when the economy gets better I think I'll be in a really good position because I've got so much experience behind me and I will have built up the framework.

I understand that you have a fiancé—a very handsome man who's been wandering around here while we've been chatting. If I were to ask him to describe the woman who he loves, what do you think he would say?

I think he'd—I don't know what he'd say. I think it's nice for a man to be with a woman who has a real sense of direction and knows what she wants to do.

What does Helen Gurley Brown say about marriage?

She got married when she was older. She was 37 the first time. She says that you shouldn't be in a rush to get married—don't rush it, which I also agree with. I think you should never get married before you're 30, and when you do get married, it's because it's what you want to do. And you should get a lot of things over with first. You should be on your own for a long time and have fun with it and get that part of your life over with so you don't regret it afterwards and feel you've missed something. I agree with that. You've got the rest of your life to be married, so why rush it?

You're soooo practical.

Am I really? I didn't mean to be. I guess I've had to be.

I tend to tell all my friends what to do. I seem to be the one with all the advice. But I never thought I was practical, maybe I am.

Revelations.

Yeah.

Ann Duggan

War is a tragedy. The end result is the suffering of countless innocent victims. To put oneself in the line of fire in order to help those who are in pain takes courage and selflessness. Ann Duggan has chosen life in a war zone to practice her profession.

Since December 1993, this 28-year-old doctor has called a small border town in Azerbaijan home. At night, she can hear the shelling between the Azerbaijanis and their Armenian neighbors, as the war that started six years ago continues.

The process of reaching Ann for our phone interview was something of a challenge. After a series of telexes between Toronto and the office of Médecins Sans Frontières/Doctors Without Borders in Baku, the capital of Azerbaijan, Ann agreed to drive 300 kilometres to a private phone at that office and await my call—if I could get through on their less-than-reliable phone system. To Ann's amazement, after just a few attempts we connected. Initially, it was difficult for the two of us to relate, since our surroundings were so different. I was sitting in the comfort and safety of my home, my cat purring at my feet. She was sitting in a stark room miles away from her family and friends, with the potential of violence and death literally down the road.

It was a far cry from simpler days in Newfoundland, where Ann was raised. Aside from the emotional pain from her parents' divorce, she grew up a regular, healthy kid in St. John's. Visits to the doctor were few and far between. When a checkup was absolutely necessary, she found it to be uncomfortable. In fact, Ann admits she had never met a doctor she liked. Based on these few experiences as she grew up, it obviously never occurred to her to enter the medical profession. But time has a way of changing the way our lives turn out.

Ann initially had aspirations to enter the theatre, so she found herself volunteering in a Planned Parenthood traveling theatre company performing skits about birth control, safe sex and peer pressure in high schools. By the time she was 16 years old, Ann was volunteering at Planned Parenthood, counseling other young women about teenage sexuality. Before she realized what was happening, her interest in theatre had waned while her desire to help grew.

After finishing high school in Ottawa, where she had moved with her father, Ann took a degree in biology at the University of Ottawa. This was followed by medical school at Queen's University, where she graduated in 1990. Then it was back to Newfoundland to do her residency in family practice. In the midst of becoming a practicing doctor, Ann was bitten by the travel bug, so she conveniently combined the two. Since finishing her residency, Ann has already worked in a number of rural communities across Canada and Central America. In November 1993, Ann joined the organization Doctors Without Borders, and has been working with them in Azerbaijan since then.

From the perspective of living in an area where people are ravaged physically and emotionally in the daily onslaught of war, Ann is quite outspoken about how lucky we are to live in Canada. Yet while we talked for two hours, connected only by a telephone wire, it crossed my mind how fortunate Ann was to be experiencing the way of life she has chosen. Living here is safe, secure and somewhat selfish. Ann Duggan, on the other hand, is spending her days helping, curing and caring for others.

I realize this is going to be a challenging interview, because here I am, safe and sound in Canada, while you're working in Azerbaijan where there's a war going on. Let's begin by locating where you are geographically.

Right now I'm in the capital of Azerbaijan, Baku, just north of Iran. Azerbaijan is on the Caspian Sea, but where I normally work is about four hours west of here, near the front line of the on-going war with Armenia.

Wow. So you're not at home right now? You traveled for four hours to do this interview?

I usually come into town three or four days every two weeks for meetings, because I'm the medical co-ordinator of the projects here, so I have meetings in the capital.

Can you describe where you live for me?

Okay, well I live in the town of Barda. It's a town of approximately 120,000 people—that's its regular population. It also has an extra 92,000 displaced people there right now, because of the areas in Azerbaijan that have been taken over by the Armenians. The country has lost about 25 per cent of its land mass, resulting in about 700,000 displaced people within the country. The town that we live in is about 35 kilometres from the front line, so it's not uncommon to hear shelling.

The town itself was shelled once, but we do hear it quite frequently, and it's fairly common that we see war-wounded soldiers in the civilian hospital here. Physically, the town is an incredibly ugly place. It's basically a dirt road with lots of dust and lots and lots of people.

What's your home like?

The house is actually—it's very exciting, because as of yesterday, I have my own bedroom. That's very exciting.

Oh, congratulations.

There are so many extra people in Barda and to find good housing is a problem, so we've had horrible battles trying to find a place to live. Heating is a huge problem, we've had a very cold winter. Most of the houses are heated by gas, and the gas pressure is usually quite low. We only have electricity intermittently, so we can't really have electrical heaters. We have kerosene heaters, but most of the kerosene is very watered down, so the heaters don't work. Heating can be a big problem.

I would assume this is a problem also in your job in the hospitals.

It's a big problem in the hospitals. The patients stay at home because they don't have heat in the hospitals and they also can't provide food any more. A lot of the hospitals are empty. It's because there just isn't the money to buy food for patients, so most people stay at home unless they're really in bad circumstances.

There's a war going on there, so can you explain briefly the reason for the conflict?

The conflict is basically between the Armenians and the Azerbaijani over who is the rightful owner of an area of land called Nargorno-Karabach. It's an enclave that was owned by Azerbaijan. But the majority of the people who were living in that area were of Armenian descent. Back around 1989, the enclave decided to announce its independence and was going to join Armenia, and the fighting began then and has been continuing since. The Armenians right now have taken Nargorno-Karabach, but also have advanced into areas beyond that enclave into traditional Azerbaijani land, and now occupy, like I say, about 25 per cent of what Azerbaijan was, six or seven years ago. And this has all happened since 1988–89. Basically, it's over this particular piece of land. Nobody really quite knows what's going to happen, because the Armenians have taken what they said they were going to take, and more, but they don't seem to want to stop the war. There was a recent cease-fire agreement in Moscow just a couple of weeks ago, but that's been broken, the fighting continuing, and nobody knows what end point people are going for any more.

Lots of fighting, but no one's advancing.

Yeah.

Let's talk a bit about yourself. You're 28 now, the eldest of two sisters and a brother. If I gave them the opportunity to describe you, what would they say?

I think they probably would all say that I'm a typical eldest child, and that I can be very stubborn and pig-headed and very controlling.

Do you have any strong childhood memories, good or bad, about a time that really helped mold who you are?

I think Newfoundlanders are traditionally very generous and very giving to areas that need money or need support. I have strong memories of visiting my grandparents' house when I was young—my father came from a family of miners and he was the first one ever to attend university. They came from quite a poor family. There were seven children and the two parents and they lived in a three-bedroom house—a parents' room, a boys' room and a girls' room, and there was a kitchen and that was it, and they had an outhouse in the back yard. I can clearly remember visiting them many times as a child—being amazed that people could live that way and work and function, go on and achieve a really good thing. I was always very inspired by that—what my grandparents had gone through, and what they had sacrificed for their kids.

Now, with all the traveling, you see much worse.

But I hadn't when I was ten years old.

When you were 14, your parents divorced. You moved in with your dad in Ottawa. That must have been very difficult—you were leaving your mom and you were a teenager leaving your friends. How did that time affect you as a person?

It was a very, very difficult time in my life but, you know, I was very involved with taking care of my younger brother and sister, and sort of helping run our house, so that's where I put all of my time and energy.

What was it like being raised by your dad?

I always tell my father I wasn't raised by him, I raised him. You know, it was completely new for him, too. He wasn't used to raising children and he had four to take care of. That was a big job, and then, of course, he had his life, too, and work in a new city, so it was very difficult for him, and I think I appreciate that more now as I get older than I did then.

What did your mom teach you?

Well, I think we were really fortunate when we were growing up—my mother was quite involved with the women's movement and so a lot of our growing up was around women's centers and rape-crisis centers, and I saw the things that can happen to people. I was very aware of the position that you might end up in if you didn't learn to take care of yourself. My mother left school when she was 16 and she got married when she was 19, and she had all of us shortly thereafter. She always told us that the most important thing was to get an education, that we had to be able to take care of ourselves, that we should never, ever be dependent on any other person for anything, in the sense of our livelihood. She taught us that we had to go to school, that we had to have some sort of career that would enable us to be able to take care of ourselves. I think some of the choices she made in her life were not only because, you know, society expected her to get married and have children, but also because she didn't have other options open to her in order to have money. In order to eat and survive, she had to marry somebody who would take care of her. And then, when my parents divorced when she was in her mid-30s, she all of a sudden had absolutely no marketable skills. She had nothing that she could go out and get a paying job with, because all of her experience had been taking care of people and doing lots of really good volunteer work, but nothing that she had been paid for. So all of those things eventually taught me valuable lessons for what I wanted to be. When I was growing up, I always knew that I had to find something to do that not only was rewarding, but also something that would enable me to make the decisions that I wanted to make in my life rather than making them because I was hungry, or I needed clothes, or I needed something, or I needed to depend on somebody else for that.

In a way, do you think your mom was teaching you the basics of what feminism is?

Definitely! You know, I think today a lot of people consider feminism to be a bad word. For me, it's not. For me, feminism is men being considered equal to women, or vice versa. My mom taught me about not being dependent on anybody else, particularly on men. And that, I think, is part of feminism too, being able to make your own independent decisions based on what you want.

Why do you think that feminism has become a bad word?

I think that some people perceive it to be bad because when they think of feminism, they think of very radical people who aren't feminists at all, they're actually people who hate men. Some people think that those two things are synonymous, when they have nothing whatsoever to do with each other. A lot of women who are feminists don't consider themselves as falling into that category. I used to have this disagreement with people in medical school all the time, because many of the women in my class would adamantly say that they weren't feminists. And I said, 'Well, how can you not be a feminist—you're here, you're in medical school, you feel like you have every right to be here, you feel like you're just as good as any of the men in your class, and you've got just as much talent and ability and intelligence and you can go anywhere that you want to go and you're a woman, so that automatically makes you a feminist.' They would agree with all of those statements—they'd agree that they had all of those skills and abilities and they had every right to do what they wanted to do, but they still wouldn't acknowledge that as being feminism. So I think it's become a bad word because people don't really look at what it actually means any more.

What did you learn from your dad that was different from what your mom taught you?

The one thing I remember about my dad is how he treated my friends when I brought them home. It was always really good, because he never, ever would say anything bad about my friends, particularly my boyfriends who I brought home when I was a teenager.

He would always just sort of accept them and tolerate them, and be polite to them, because he always said to me, 'You know, you have to make your decisions, you're intelligent and you have to live with the choices that you make, and I trust you to make good choices.' I always respected that—that he treated me in that way. And then later, after I decided that a particular boyfriend wasn't good, then he'd always say, 'Oh, I never liked him anyway.' It was really, really good that he never tried to run my life. He always let me make the choices and see the natural conclusions of those choices without interfering too much. I think that's a very difficult thing to do as a parent, but a very important thing to do also, as long as you feel like, you know, your teenager's not going to get into too much trouble because of the choices they're making.

Exactly. You credit your teenage involvement with the Planned Parenthood organization with your decision to become a doctor. And you also connect your love of theatre with Planned Parenthood. Can you explain how all these interests mesh?

Yeah, it's all very complicated. You know, when I was a teenager, 14, 15, I was very enthralled with the theatre. I was involved in a lot of different plays and acting. It happened that when I turned 16, Planned Parenthood ran a theatre group and they asked people to audition for this improvisational group. It consisted of about ten or 15 teenagers between the ages of 15 and 18. There was a collection of skits on general topics that were improvised. The group traveled around to different high schools and teenage community centres every week. I got involved because I really enjoyed theatre and I thought the topics they were dealing with were really interesting. I'd had the history of being involved with women's centres, growing up as a child. I went and auditioned for them and I was given a part. I spent that whole year of high school taking one afternoon off a week and going to some other high school to do the improvisational skit, and it was a really, really wonderful experience—you know, being up there and acting, because I enjoyed acting a lot. But also just for things that we were dealing with and what we were portraying. We did stuff on teen suicide, birth control, pregnancy, abortion, smoking, peer pressure, drinking, everything, all sorts of topics. I think people enjoyed watching it, and we used to have really deep discussions afterwards. I felt like I was doing something useful and worthwhile. I continued my involvement with Planned Parenthood after I was in the theatre group, I continued on as a volunteer and I had a summer job with them. I continued doing more peer counseling and it was a wonderfully rewarding experience. It sounds hokey, but I was doing something useful for other people and that made me feel good. I decided to continue on in that area, and I just had to think about different alternatives for continuing on in that line of work. It was useful because that was all happening at the time when I was trying to decide about university and what I was going to do, and that made the decision a lot easier, because I was so interested in that area.

And so from acting you became a doctor.

Yeah, I seriously considered doing a theatre degree instead of going into biology, but biology won out.

So did you know in medical school that your residency would be in family medicine?

No. No. When I first applied to medical school I thought I would do obstetrics, delivering babies, because I was very interested in the area of sexuality and birth control. Because of my involvement with Planned Parenthood I was very comfortable in that area. I thought that I'd go on and specialize in that area. Then, through medical school, I realized that I still loved obstetrics, but I also became aware of other areas of medicine and decided that I enjoyed them, too. I got quite involved in adolescent health issues with regards to counseling. I also realized that to go into the special fields of obstetrics and gynecology required a lot of surgery, it's a lot of technical, very specialized types of things. Whereas if you're going into family practice, you have contact with different people, you get to do counseling, plus you get to deliver babies too. So, you get a lot of rewarding things. When I'm in Canada, obviously a vast majority of my patients are teenage females and many of them are coming for birth control, which is great, from my perspective. I like it when a teenager comes to me and she's being responsible and she's coming asking for birth control, because it shows that they're really putting a lot of thought into their future and a lot of thought into what they're doing, and it's taking responsibility for the choices that they're making, and that's great. Of course, I also deal with a lot of teenage females who haven't really seen it right through that clearly and are coming to me pregnant, trying to figure out what their options are at that point.

I've heard horrifying tales of the extreme work load that student doctors, interns and residents have to carry. Is it true?

It definitely is true. Going through medical school is quite difficult, but I think anybody who wants to do it can do it, you just have to work very, very hard. You have to realize that the hours are long. You know, anybody can do it. But as an intern, particularly, it's very, very long hours and, you know, you're often up working 36 hours straight, doing all sorts of different things. It's definitely intense work, much harder than what I'm doing now for sure.

Why do they keep you up for 36 hours at a time?

The theory is that you have to be able to work under duress, you have to be able to think quickly and act quickly even when you're tired and be able to respond to, you know, emergency situations and everyday ones when they come up. That's what we're told. Also that we need a broad spectrum of clinical exposure and the really interesting cases, the difficult medical problems, they're always in the middle of the night, they're never in the middle of the day.

Why?

If people are going to have car accidents or if people are going to get really sick, it does tend to be in the middle of the night. People tend to have babies in the middle of the night. So there certainly is some validity to working nights, but the number of nights we have to work I think is a little bit ridiculous. For myself, I think that it's definitely too much in many different ways, because once you're past a certain stage and your level of fatigue is high, you know, you don't learn any more anyway, and you certainly can then become a danger to the people who you're working with, rather than a health service, which is what you're trying to be.

Did you ever feel that you weren't going to make it?

There were many times that I thought, 'Why am I doing this?' But whenever that came up, whenever I felt really, really sick, I always thought, 'I'm doing this because this is what I really want to do, and in the end it is going to be worth it. I'm going to be able to work at a job that I'm going to want to do, I'm going to be able to get a good salary and I'm going to be able to help other people.' And I think what's important is that no matter what you're doing, you remember why it is you're doing it.

Which leads me to the next question. What advice can you offer young women wishing to become doctors?

For any young woman wanting to be a doctor, I would say that it's a wonderful career. You can do many, many good things by being a physician, and if you want to do it, you can do it, but you should remember why it is that you want to do it and just keep thinking about that and keep working for it. So when it comes to all those exams in high school, and it comes to studying, and it comes to doing your homework, and it comes to working very, very hard, you always have to remember your end goal and just keep working for that. That's what I did and it proved to work very well for me.

Talking to you on the phone, you sound unbelievably pragmatic. It seems to me that you simply decide you want to do something, and then you just do it.

I just do it.

You make decisions sound so simple. Are they?

Yeah. One thing that I hate in the world is people who whine and people who make excuses for things. But for me—if I decide that I want to do something, then I think about how I can accomplish it and then I work for it. I think the most important thing is deciding what it is that you want, and then once you know what you want, the rest of it is easy. It's so easy to make up excuses about why you can't do something, but you know, people can achieve anything, they can obtain anything that they want, as long as they put their minds to it. And people in Canada are so fortunate, almost everyone has heat in their house, and they have running water, and they have electricity, and they have food in their bellies, and have schools to go to. The thing is, they have to focus on what they have, what the good things are. And they have so many—such a strong base to go on and do other things with, to accomplish the things they want to do.

And then go for it, because the avenues that are open, the goals that can be achieved are so tremendous, completely different from a place like the Philippines or Guyana or Guatemala, where they don't even have food, so they can't think of the same goals and the same dreams that we have the ability to work for.

What percentage of graduates in your class were female?

About one-third.

Did you or any of the females in your class experience any gender bias during training?

Oh, there certainly is gender bias during training. I was a representative on the gender issues committee for two years at our university. There certainly were gender issues, mostly with regards to gender stereotyping in our technical courses—some of the older male professors who still had some pretty stereotypical views on how women should be treated. It wasn't severe, most of the people that I worked with were at least trying to be gender equal. But I can remember being told one day by one professor that he thought it would be good if I became a radiologist, because radiologists had good nine-to-five working hours and they always got their weekends off, and that was a really good type of profession for a woman to have. I can remember being very annoyed about that, because it certainly was not my image of what I wanted to be like as a doctor—working nine to five and never working weekends. The idea that I would want to do that just because I was a woman upset me a lot.

He'd be shaking his head in disbelief if he knew what you were doing right now, living and working 35 kilometres from a war zone.

I think he'd think I was totally insane.

You're working in countries where women have less rights than they do in Canada.

Oh, definitely. This is a Moslem country that I'm working in, so women have relatively few rights here at all. It's a bit difficult to take sometimes, but it's also very interesting. I had one little child come up to me on the street the other day, a little three-year-old, and she said to me, 'Are you a boy or a girl? Why are you wearing pants?' It was the first time that I realized none of the women here wear pants, they all wear skirts, and I'd been wearing pants ever since I arrived here and I hadn't been aware of it. It just totally took me by surprise.

Do you have more rights or more difficulties than men because you're a doctor? What's their reaction to you?

I think I do have more difficulties than my male colleagues here because I am a woman, particularly being a co-ordinator of this program.

Meaning that you're essentially the boss?

Yeah. Most of the local people, local men, don't easily accept that. One of my colleagues who I work with here is a man and he's 53, so they automatically assume that he is the one in charge. They don't understand how it could be possible that I'm the co-ordinator and he is my colleague, that essentially I am his boss. They have a very difficult time understanding that, because it's not part of their culture. I think they are quite used to having women physicians here. It's quite an interesting culture that way, women physicians are quite common, but they are usually obstetricians, because it's considered a female specialty. So to be a doctor and to be female is not unusual. But to be a doctor and to be the co-ordinator, and to wear pants and just sort of generally go where you want to go is quite unusual.

You said that you have never met a doctor that you much liked when you were growing up. How did that affect the kind of doctor that you've become?

When I was growing up, I didn't think very much of doctors at all. I mean, doctors were men in white coats who usually did very painful things to you. In my family, we were never a sickly family. I mean, you didn't go to the doctor unless you were on death's door. So I never had much contact with the medical system at all. When I was considering entering medicine, I realized that I didn't really know any doctors. I didn't have any role models at all. And I certainly didn't know any female doctors at that point. But still, somehow I knew that was what I wanted to do.

I don't wear a white coat. I haven't worn a white coat since medical school, because I feel like that image of wearing a white coat is a very sterile, artificial image that physicians use to try and separate themselves from people, and somehow try and make themselves on a different level from their patients. I don't feel it's to the doctor's advantage, particularly when you are working with children. It's very scary for them. Also when you're working with teenagers and little kids, it's good to talk at their level, as intelligent, equal human beings. I always talk to all of my patients, you know, as equals. I don't think anybody's been scared of me. At least I hope not.

Here's a quote I found from Katherine Butler Hathaway, who wrote this in the 1940s: 'A person needs at intervals to separate himself from family and companions, and go to new places. He must go without his familiars in order

to be open to influences to change.' How does that apply to you?

I would agree with that, except that she's very sexist. Change that 'he' to 'they.' I think that's very true. A lot of people, when they have their normal life they can become very comfortable with it, with their family and their friends and what they're doing. It's something secure and it's something that they know, but to really grow and to really expand and to learn more about the world—and especially more about yourself—you need to separate yourself from the familiar and go out and explore, look at other things. Because life can become very, very comfortable when you're in a safe place.

How has practicing medicine so far away from home affected you—do you see yourself changing?

I think that right now, I'm essentially the same person I was when I was 14 years old. And mostly what I'm doing in places and the experiences I gather when I go just make me more and more and more aware of how lucky I've been in my life, in the upbringing that I've had and the opportunities that I've had, because I've had so many opportunities open for me. I've just become more and more aware of that.

How many different geographical areas have you practiced medicine in so far?

It's hard to say 'practice medicine.' 'Worked medically' might be a more correct term because here in Azerbaijan, I actually don't clinically practice, I don't take care of patients myself. I'm actually doing drug supply distributions to different hospitals and training their local physicians. But I don't take care of patients myself. When I was a medical student, I worked in the Philippines and in Thailand a little bit. Also as a student, I worked in Guyana in South America. Then last year, I was in Guatemala working. So I figure I have to go to Africa next. I'm missing that area.

You speak English and Spanish. How do you treat a patient if they speak neither language?

Here we work with translators and it's critical that you have a very, very good translator. Most of the other countries that I've been in either spoke English or Spanish. When I finished medical school I set as a goal that I was going to learn a second language, so I chose Spanish. That's why I went to Central America—to learn, which I did.

And when you go to Africa, what's gonna happen?

Who knows, maybe I'll learn Swahili, you never know. It just depends on what country I'm in. Here in Azerbaijan I've learned a little bit of Azeri, but it's a difficult language. It's a completely different alphabet and there aren't Azeri-English dictionaries around, so it's a difficult language to learn.

What's been your harshest medical experience to date?

One of the ones that stands out clearly in my mind was when I was in Guyana as a medical student. I was holding a little baby who was malnourished and dehydrated because of diarrhea and the baby died when I was trying to feed it. That was a very traumatic experience, because although I had been present before when people had died, I'd never actually been holding a baby in my arms, and the guilt that you feel, wondering if you might have precipitated it by trying to make the baby eat. It was a real shock for me. Being close to war zones, and also being in an environment where death is quite common—well, I think we cope with a death the same way that you cope with other horrible medical things. You know, people who've been smashed up by a drunk driver, people who've just suffered horrible losses, you get a kind of shell around you, not an impermeable one, but a flexible one where you try to distance yourself so that you don't take it personally, you try to see it as something outside of yourself. Sometimes people fault doctors for that—for not seeming to care and for not being able to really understand what's going on. But it's not that at all, for myself anyway, because you do have to distance yourself from it in order to continue to work and in order to cope and to function. If you felt every death or every trauma personally, you'd go insane.

Has that been balanced by a specific, joyful, satisfying experience?

You know, there are many joyful experiences in medicine. That's why I really enjoy medicine—you feel satisfied that you've really helped somebody, that you've made a difference for them. You know, when you deliver a healthy baby—help deliver it, help the baby, because of course the woman does all the work, you certainly don't. When you come to some of these developing countries or war-torn countries and you're able to give medical aid to people who otherwise wouldn't be receiving it, that's a very fulfilling experience.

How did you get involved with doctors who do that kind of work?

When I was working in Guyana, when I was a medical student, I met some people from Médecins sans Frontières and I was very impressed with how they worked and how they ran the organization. I always thought that once I was finished medical school and had some experience, that was something I would really like to get involved with myself.

What's their mandate?

Basically it's to help provide medical aid to anyone who needs it, regardless of race, religion, nationality, or which side in the war zone they happen to be on. Anybody who is in need of medical care deserves to get it, and they will help provide it—that's their basic philosophy. That appeals to me a lot, you know, that everybody has the basic right to medical care. So after I finished my residency, I decided I needed to get some experience working in rural Canada and I needed to learn a second language, and so I did that, and then I decided it was time to work overseas and go to an area of the world that needed medical assistance, and that's how I ended up here.

Did you choose this location, or were you placed here?

No, I didn't choose it. It's how MSF works. It has projects in many different countries in the world—about 200 countries, I believe. They assess you and offer you a position they think is appropriate for you, and then you say yes or no. This was the place that I was offered, so I said, 'Sure.' I'm willing to go anywhere and try anything once.

But it seems that in working with MSF, you've found the best of both your worlds: the medical one and the travel one.

Yeah, it's very good combo. I have the medical aspects, the travel aspects and the other aspect is that it's very good for me as emergency medical relief. It's short-term projects, so I can work for six months with them and then go back to Canada and work for two or three months up in the north of Canada, or in some other areas of Canada, and do the type of medicine that I find is very rewarding there, and then I can go to another project. So it's perfect for me.

So what are the pleasures of this particular job?

Hmm. In Azerbaijan specifically? We are able to provide hospitals and physicians with what they wouldn't otherwise have, and these are hospitals that right now are sitting empty—they have no heat, there's no food, there's very little electricity, there's very little medication or supplies to do anything. So there are doctors and nurses sitting in the hospital who can't work. We come and give them some supplies—essentially give them the ability to get back to work and start caring, taking care of the patients in their area. So there's the satisfaction of knowing you're helping that physician in that hospital get working again. It's also the satisfaction of knowing that the population in that area will receive basic medical care again, which they haven't been receiving because the war has affected the economy and the country itself can no longer supply these essential medicines and supplies to the hospital. Hopefully, if the war ends, the economy will improve and the regular system will take over again.

You're 35 kilometres away from a war zone. Doesn't war scare you?

Of course, war is a very scary thing, war's a horrible thing. You know, when you see these people who have lost their arms and their legs or have been killed because of a war, it's a very scary, horrible thing. It's—you know, I don't really understand why it is that people continue to engage in this sort of thing, because it really is foolish and history has shown us that we don't accomplish very much with war. But for myself, I don't feel threatened or consider myself in any danger here at all. I'm actually very, very fortunate. Because I'm a foreigner, people treat me with respect and they treat me well, and I know that I won't be endangered on purpose. Sometimes it's a little concerning because you think, 'Well, a stray shell might be anywhere.' But it's something that I really don't think too much about. Certainly people in Sarajevo and other areas of the world are in a lot more danger.

Let me paint a picture for you. All right, it's one of those days when your water is off, no heat and your electricity is cut off, and you can hear shelling not too far away, and there's a busload of wounded that has just entered one of the hospitals that have no water, etcetera, etcetera. So, you know all this is happening, you've passed out your medical supplies, you've done your training—there's not much you can do at this point. You're lying in bed that night. What gets you through these tough times?

Usually if I'm lying in bed, I'm fast asleep. As long as you're doing the best that you can, then you can feel good about yourself and what you're doing, and you just keep thinking that—you just keep on thinking, 'What am I doing here and am I achieving my goals?' As long as I can keep telling myself that I'm achieving my goals, then I'm happy, then the no heat, no water, no electricity don't bother me at all.

What about relationships with men? How do they fit into your lifestyle?

It's interesting, because when I was growing up, I always had a regular boyfriend, long-term relationships, and then when I got to the end of my medical training, I got sort of finished, and since then it hasn't really been a priority. You know, my priorities right now are to travel and to work overseas and to do all these things that I wanted to do for so long. That's my number one goal, and so relationships have taken a back seat to that. You do have intermittent relationships—with the nature of the work they tend to be short-term. And, you know, you do meet people, and that's one thing that a lot of my female friends who are doctors back home say, 'You're never gonna meet anybody, you're never gonna get married if you just keep traveling, and working, and doing all these crazy things.'

And I keep telling them, 'When I'm traveling and working in these crazy places, I meet much more interesting people than I'd ever meet sitting in Ottawa.'

Right. Now, I want you to think ahead 30 years. Your daughter or your son is also a doctor working where there is war going on. And you are living back in Canada. How well would you be sleeping at night?

I'd probably be scared to death. I'm sure my father is right now. Of course, if my son or daughter were working in a war zone, I'd be very nervous and scared and worried about them. But I'd also have a lot of respect for them because I would know that they would be doing what they wanted to do, and I would encourage that. And I think that it's important that parents always encourage their kids to do what they want, and to choose the goals they want to pursue even if it's not something that the parents may choose to do themselves. I have a lot of respect for my father because he still supports me and encourages me, even though I know he would much rather I was back home in Canada, but he keeps that to himself, and I appreciate that.

What's the best advice you've ever received that has almost become a philosophy of yours?

Hmm. The best advice I've ever received was from my mother and that's that I can be whatever I want to be. That I can accomplish whatever I want to accomplish, and that's always been the best advice. There's always been something that I've reached for. Every time I wanted to be something, every time I think about something, I tell myself that if I want it, I can do it. I just have to work hard enough and keep that goal in mind. I think that's so important—for people to believe in themselves, to believe in their abilities. That's the best advice I've ever gotten. And luckily I've been able to incorporate that into who I am.

Nathalie Karvonen

When 27-year-old Nathalie Karvonen opened the Toronto Wildlife Centre, she single-handedly took on the huge responsibility of protecting wildlife in the greater Toronto area. The Centre's mandate is to care for any sick, injured or orphaned animals, birds and reptiles.

After a year and a half in operation, the facility is already bursting at the seams, forcing Nathalie to find a new, larger home for her menagerie. The scene of the Centre's big move would probably bring to mind Noah's story from the Bible, as he loaded up his ark with every species of animal imaginable to protect them from divine extinction.

Nathalie Karvonen has always had a soft spot for any living creature. From the time she was quite young, she was more interested in playing with the animals that she found and dragged home than playing with other kids. Painfully shy, she found herself most comfortable with the feathered or furry friends that she befriended every summer at her family's cottage. What was initially a childhood pastime slowly became an all-consuming fascination with the animal kingdom. Nathalie set out to learn anything and everything she could about wildlife. It began with a high-school biology award. The next step was an Honors Bachelor of Science degree in biology from the University of Guelph. For the next four years while Nathalie studied at university, she spent all her free time doing volunteer and part-time work learning to care for animals.

The variety of jobs that Nathalie has already had in her field adds up to years of experience. She started off volunteering as a veterinarian's assistant. At the same time she gave talks to the public about wild animals at the Metro Toronto Zoo, which led to a volunteer position at the Wild Bird Clinic at the Ontario Veterinary College. The following summer, Nathalie moved on to bigger things, literally, with a job at the African Lion Safari, coming in daily contact with cheetahs, lions, tigers, rhinos, giraffes and baboons. But nothing is bigger than an elephant, as Nathalie found out when she was almost crushed by one the following summer working at the zoo.

After graduation, it was time to look for a full-time job. Based on her impressive résumé, she landed a position with the Toronto Humane Society, where she spent two years absorbing everything she could about wildlife rehabilitation. All these skills, combined with an incredible drive and ability to focus, are what made it possible for Nathalie to undertake the huge project of opening up the Toronto Wildlife Centre.

The Centre officially opened its doors in March 1993. Since then, virtually thousands of God's little creatures have been rehabilitated by Nathalie and her team of volunteers. The responsibility is relentless. Animals are brought in at all times of the night and day, and, like a doctor on call, if an animal is hurt and needs help, Nathalie or someone on staff has to be there. In retrospect, she had no idea just how much work would be required to keep the Centre going. From fundraising, to training volunteers, to building cages, to establishing a network of emergency rescue drivers—even to changing the city's zoning laws, Nathalie does it all, with little thanks from the critters she cares for.

The demands on her time are so great that this interview almost didn't happen. At two o'clock in the afternoon, when she was supposed to be at my home, the phone rang with a panicked Nathalie on the line, explaining that she would have to cancel our meeting because an owl with a broken wing had just been brought in and her volunteer had called in sick and there was no one to take care of the situation. You get the picture. Needless to say, the interview did eventually get done, albeit a couple of hours late, after Nathalie mended the owl's wing, tracked down another volunteer and made sure that all the animals were safe and secure.

I know that you have a warehouse full of injured and homeless animals, but what about at home? Do you have a lot of pets?

Well, I don't think I have a lot of pets. I don't have a dog, I have only one cat. Part of that is the cat's choice, because she's Siamese and she will not allow another cat in the house. But still, I don't think I would want another cat. I have two ferrets and then I have a lot of other animals that just sort of do their own thing. I have four turtles that were dumped on me when I was working at the Humane Society and they're in a kiddy wading pool. I built them a land area and they've got a heat lamp that comes on with a timer and they don't really care as long as the turtle food's there. I also have three ring-necked doves that were also dumped on me when I was at the Humane Society, and they have their flight cage and I let them out to fly around the room. And I have one fish I'm trying to find an appropriate home for, because I refuse to let it go to a pet store. I hate the whole thing about how they get these fish in pet stores, so I'm not going to buy him a friend, but I'm trying to get him a friend to put him in with. And I have three frogs that were rescued from a university experiment when I was in school.

How old are your frogs?

My frogs are seven, six.

You've had these same frogs for seven years?

Yes, and I've asked people what their life span is—frog people, my frog contacts—and they think about five years, but it's seven now, so.... I don't do anything for them. They're quiet, they have a big tank and they just hang there on the glass looking out at me from this tank. When they go into mating season, the little male courts the big fat females around the tank.

Do they have a lot of babies?

Once I made the mistake that when they started the breeding ritual, I let them go through the breeding and then took the eggs out and put them in a separate tank, so that the parents wouldn't eat them—because that's what they normally do with the eggs. I thought they really weren't going to hatch, but they did! And I had to find homes for 130 frogs! So the next time they had eggs, I left them and—have a good time, eat your eggs.

The problem is that you make them so healthy, they don't die. When do you have time for a personal life?

Not very often. It's a little better in the winter time. I think—I hope—things are going to be changing a lot at the Toronto Wildlife Centre. Because we just opened last March. Last summer was complete madness. I worked way more than I knew was healthy to work, but I didn't have a whole lot of choice. When you're running an organization that has to do with injured animals, you can't just close up and take a couple of days off. You're sort of stuck there unless someone else can take over for you and, because we were new, there were very few volunteers who had enough background that I could comfortably leave and know that everything was okay. So I didn't have much time for a personal life last summer. I have a little bit of time now—a couple of evenings a week I could do something if I had money enough to do it, but I don't.

Your parents must be very proud of what you're doing with the Wildlife Centre.

My parents are very proud of me—they've both told me that. They're both very supportive of what I'm doing, although they're not really 'animal' people, you know. They don't dislike animals, but they're very neutral about animals. If it wasn't for me, they probably wouldn't have any animals in the house and, growing up, they didn't have any animals in the house. Then they got stuck with this daughter who brought home everything. So they don't wish any harm upon them, but I think, when I was younger, they used to think, 'This is getting a bit much.' Because I was dragging home everything. It's better now. But I think they're very proud of what I'm doing.

So you were the kind of kid who brought home all kinds of critters?

Yes. I would bring home snakes, frogs, stray cats. I remember once we had this stray cat who came around. He'd been in some kind of fight—he was all bleeding and beaten up—he looked really horrible. At this stage, I would take it to an emergency clinic right away, but then I was just a little kid and my parents wouldn't let it in the house—this big, flea-bitten, dirty, stray cat. So I snuck out of the house and slept in the garage with the cat overnight, because I was so worried about this cat not being allowed in the house. I was always bringing home animals. I'd build these boxes for the cats out in the back yard—or for anything else that came around.

I understand that you grew up in the city, so where did your love for wildlife come from?

I grew up in the city, but we do have a cottage in the Kawarthas. In fact, my dad grew up there. They got it in the late 1940s—my grandparents got it. We used to go up there every single weekend. It's on a little island in the middle of the lake in the wilderness—there's still no running water and there's only electricity in one little building, but it's so beautiful up there and there's wildlife everywhere, so I'm sure that had a lot to do with it.

You and your two sisters are all animal lovers. That's kind of interesting—that animals are not your parents' main interest, yet your sisters headed in the same direction.

Well, I'm the oldest and I think that my sisters were really exposed to a lot of animals through me, growing up. They really didn't have many pets of their own—I brought them into the house and so they were always inadvertently surrounded by animals.

One of your sisters is an animal activist. I understand that her beliefs are quite extreme.

Like most animal-rights activists—she's anti-fur and anti–eating meat and anti–animal testing. She protests against all of those kinds of things, and she does a lot of volunteer work for the Wildlife Centre, but I always have to say to her, when she's doing volunteer work, 'Remember that this is a different organization.' If someone comes up perhaps wearing a fur coat, she shouldn't throw paint. And she's been pretty good about that.

When you hear about animal-rights activists doing things like throwing paint on fur coats, what are your reactions?

My sister and I talk about this all the time, and I think that I agree with most of the things they believe, although not to the same extreme. For example, with the fur coat issue, my grandmother, who's in her mid-80s, she has a fur coat that she's had for maybe 65 years. She comes from Finland and they lived on a farm, it's freezing in Finland. And that's what everybody wore in Finland. It wasn't a matter of fashion, it was a matter of living in a freezing climate. Yet if somebody came up and threw paint on her, I would be livid. That's a lot different than maybe someone who's our age and is more educated about where these animals are coming from and the options that they have and, in the case of some particular types of fur, all the suffering that goes on. That's a lot different than older people who have had furs for a long time. But if you're an extreme person like some of the animal-rights activists are—not all of them—they don't make that differentiation. They don't really allow for the gray areas.

Do you consider yourself an activist?

No, I don't consider myself an activist. I support my sister in what she does, but I don't agree with some of their methods. Also, the Toronto Wildlife Centre revolves around me so much and we are a registered charity—registered charities are prohibited from political lobbying. A lot of the activities that animal-rights activists do are prohibited by law for registered charities to do, and so I can't go out there and get arrested and get into trouble and still maintain my position at the Wildlife Centre.

Are you a vegetarian?

I'm sort of vegetarian. There are some kinds of meat I don't eat. I still eat seafood and I still sometimes eat chicken—it's sort of a very 'I'm thinking about it a lot right now' issue. There are definitely some things I don't eat. I think, for me, the biggest factor is factory farming. I almost never eat meat of any kind, but once in a while I still do. I think it's because of my background in biology. I know that we are meant to be carnivorous animals and we are meant to eat meat as part of our diet. But these animals aren't meant to be raised in the conditions that they're being raised in. I'm sort of tossing these issues back and forth right now.

It's hard to be black and white, though. When you say you're a vegetarian, that's 100 per cent one way, and then if you have a little diversion—you have the chicken—you're a hypocrite.

Usually if people ask me about something that I'm ordering or not ordering, I won't enter into a conversation about it. 'Why aren't you ordering veal?' I'm just not going to—I don't want to sit there for three hours and argue about it. I just want to eat it.

What's been your most unusual case that's been brought into the Centre so far, since it's opened?

Probably the six baby squirrels that were all tied together by the tail. That was pretty unusual.

What's the story behind that?

We don't really know. They were found in the middle of a yard like that. They weren't tiny babies—they were juveniles that would normally have been running around on their own. All their tails were tied together in this knot of wire. It was hard to tell if it had been done intentionally or if, somehow, they'd gotten like that some other way. But it did seem that someone had tied them.

How do you feel when a case like that is brought in?

I feel very, very angry. It makes me so upset that people don't respect things until they're endangered or even extinct. You have to respect living creatures when they're actually here. Like the members of your family—you have to enjoy and respect them while they're here. Just because an animal is common doesn't mean that it's not valuable or it's not interesting. It's just—it drives me crazy. People have this attitude that squirrels and pigeons are all over the place, so let's do what we want to them. And some of the things that people do are really, really cruel.

And you see most of them.

We see a lot of them, and I think we will see more and more as we go on and as we get bigger and better known. That's something I'm not really looking forward to, but then, in a way, I am, because every time something like that comes in, I'm going to go to the media and say, 'Look what someone's done this time' and maybe try to get some attention and some education for the public out of things like that. And get people angry about it so they'll watch each other and see what's going on.

Toronto's never before had an organization devoted to the care of sick and injured wildlife. Then in 1991 you—a 24-year-old—came along and took on this huge responsibility by founding the Toronto Wildlife Centre. What do you think made people believe in you and your cause?

Actually, one of the reasons I did it at that point in my life was because I thought about the connections I might have or the favors I might be able to call in at that time. I thought I had enough of them that it might work. I had sort of dabbled in a few areas here and there, I had maintained those connections. For example, at the Zoo and at the University of Guelph. I had made an effort to go to these wildlife conferences and made connections through them so that I would have people to get information from, if I needed it. It would have been very hard to start from scratch, not knowing who to call for help or advice. There were a lot of great people who I was able to call and say, 'Can you help me?' And I still have them. I was really lucky.

When people say 'lucky' I always jump on them, because I believe that in building projects like this, luck is such a small part of things. I think, as you said, it's the fact that you built up contacts and you stuck with them and you kept in touch with them. You built a network of people to help support you in this new venture. But what I want to know is, what was your sales pitch?

I think people were receptive to it, in part, because there was such a big need for this. You could go to them and say, 'Toronto doesn't have a wildlife centre and Toronto really needs one.' We actually did a preliminary survey of organizations that everyone thinks are handling wildlife. There was a big need. So being able to go to them and explain what we're doing, then tell them what my qualifications are and tell them the qualifications of the people who are associated with me, and being able to say, 'We have the support of the Metro Toronto Zoo and we have the support of this and that veterinarian'—that lent a lot of credibility to what we were doing. Because we weren't just a group of bunny-huggers saying, 'We don't know anything but we want to do it anyway.' You have to pull their heart strings, but at the same time you have to maintain a professional attitude, so they know that you care about the animals but you're going to go about it in an efficient and professional way. That's what I have felt really strongly about and what I've pushed everyone at the Wildlife Centre to maintain. Even though they may be doing something that's all volunteer work, we have to be professional about it. Otherwise people are not going to believe we're capable of doing what we do.

You also have some very prestigious people on your board of directors. How did you get these people involved?

Some of those people were involved with the Centre before they were actually asked to be on the board. For example, the president of Aikenhead's. I was writing letters to a lot of different lumber-supply places, trying to get lumber and cage materials donated, because we had all these babies coming in and we had to make a lot of release cages to take them out to the properties where they were going to be released. These cages normally would cost hundreds of dollars to make per cage—and when you have eight big raccoons and 200 baby squirrels and all these birds—that's a lot of money in cage materials. I was sending letters to different companies and I was getting, 'No, no, no.' The letter to Aikenhead's was one of the last ones I sent. Not because I didn't believe in them, but just because of the random way that I did it. I was going to call them back in a few days and I think within ten minutes of getting the letter, he called me and said, 'You've found a wildlife lover. You can have whatever you want.' Yes! He was so great. I think maybe that was luck, in a way. Sure, I sent the letter, but....

If you sent a letter to every hardware store in the city, where's the luck? Was starting a wildlife centre a dream of yours?

Not at all. Well, it wasn't that it wasn't a dream—for one thing, I wasn't aware that there was this problem in Toronto. I didn't know anything about it. When I graduated, I knew that I was going to be working with animals because I always had and I always would. That was just a fact. But I didn't know in what capacity. So when I started doing volunteer work with wildlife, that got me really excited. That's when I started to ask the same questions other people asked, like, 'Where are the other wildlife centres?' Well, there aren't any. 'Then who's looking after the animals that go other places?' Well, they euthanize them. I was sort of—wow, don't people care? Some of these organizations—I don't want to name names, but—they're taking in animals and euthanizing them. They're taking in 2,000 to 3,000 wild animals a year. That's all different species, and the scary thing is they probably don't even recognize all the species they have. There's a lot of endangered, threatened species of birds—some, certainly, that pass through Toronto. Sometimes we'll get a bird in and it will take us an hour to identify it. I can't imagine that someone who doesn't normally make an attempt to identify birds would recognize species like that. They would just be euthanized. It's really frustrating. So I didn't have that in mind when I graduated, I sort of fell into it as I learned more about the wildlife situation in Toronto.

How important was your schooling in getting you to the point where you could open up your own wildlife centre?

My degree in biology certainly did not train me to do hands-on work in wildlife rehabilitation. It did give me a very good background in a little bit of everything. Anatomy, physiology, nutrition, biochemistry of how the bodies of many of these animals work. It made it a lot easier, I think, to learn what I did learn once I got out of school, because I was starting with a broad and solid base—basically, how these animals function and how these diseases function, how the immune system functions—all those types of things. What university did for me—and probably does for most people—is it teaches you how to learn properly. It was pretty easy—if I didn't know something, I could quickly figure out where to go, how to find out. You have your research skills to fall back on, and that helped a lot. Because every day, there's something I don't know. You can't work in a situation where any day you can get any one of 300 different species of animals of every different age and gender and medical problem and know everything about it.

There was a duck that was brought to the Centre that thought he was a dog. This is a psychological problem. Where did you learn about animal psychology?

It's something that I've definitely learned from the wildlife conferences that I go to every year. They do a lot. They always have some lectures about the psychological aspects of working with wildlife because it is so important—especially when you're working with the babies. But I think a lot of it is—you know, if you're an 'animal person' and you love animals, you're just more aware of things from the animal's perspective. If you have somebody who's a real dog lover, they'll often be able to tell in a given situation what their dog might be thinking about something. You almost get to the point where you can be like that with wildlife. A bird comes in and you look at him and you know he's terrified and he thinks you're going to eat him. So you cuddle him up and put him somewhere quiet because you want to alleviate that stress for him. It's partly learned, but partly it's just trying to figure out what's happening from the duck's perspective.

Have you ever met an animal that you didn't like?

I don't like cockroaches very much. But no, I don't think so. I find some animals more annoying to work with than others. But I think that's only because we've put them in a stressful situation. Like, for example, baboons. I worked with baboons a couple of times, and they may be lovely creatures in the wild, but if you put them in a crammed little cage and—the one place I was working, they kept them in horrid conditions. Every time you walked by the cage they would grab your hair and slam your head into the side of the cage and they'd throw rocks at you. They were sort of horrendous to work with. But I think it wasn't really their fault. I'm not going to say I don't like baboons, because I'm sure that if I saw them in their natural habitat, they'd be just fine, but because they have such great dexterity in their hands, and because they're so intelligent—if they want to do something, then they can do it very well. I went home with bruises many times.

You need a lot of patience to do what you do.

Yes, because sometimes you're in situations, especially working with wildlife, where you know you'll probably get bitten. Not very often, but if you're doing something with an animal that requires you to use your hands, and you can't wear leather gloves, and you're working somewhere near their mouth, you say to yourself, 'There's a pretty good chance I'm going to get bitten.' So you're bitten—fine—'Can someone get his teeth out of my hand?' You can't just slam him down on the floor and go, 'Get off my hand.' You have to expect it and deal with it the best you can.

Do you find sometimes that you're the kind of person who gets along with animals better than people?

Not all people, but I guess so, yes. There's a lot of people I really like but a lot of people—well, I'd rather be with an animal, that's for sure.

I find animals more predictable a lot of the time. Unless an animal has been affected by a person, I know what to expect from them. People aren't like that. You never know what to expect from a person on the street. They may turn around a month later and do some lying, conniving. Turn into an ax murderer. For someone like me—because

I think I'm quite trusting—I can't see through people like that very well. But if it's an animal, I know that if it's mad at me, it's going to raise its hair up or it's going to slash at me with its claws. But if it's a person who's mad at me, and they've been harboring this resentment for a month and they're finally going to do something—it's not the same thing.

Do you cry when you lose an animal?

Some animals I do. I have to expect that that's going to happen sometimes, and I can't—I definitely don't let myself get upset about some animals. There are some animals that come in and you almost know they have a very good chance of dying. So those animals I don't get upset about. Over the years, I've had to get this mind-set: 'Okay, we'll do the best for these animals, but don't get upset because, first thing in the morning, you go straight to the cage and you know they're probably going to be dead...and they are.' Those ones I don't cry about. I mean, I'm sad, but.... The ones that upset me are the ones that come in and they're really borderline, and you think they're going to die but they pull through, and you think, 'Wow, this little guy is a real trouper and he's getting stronger and stronger, and he's overcome some really huge obstacles' and then a couple of weeks later, suddenly, out of nowhere, bang, he'll just drop dead. Those ones are so hard. You let yourself think, 'This animal's going to be fine' and it's a surprise—you're not emotionally prepared for those animals to die. Those are the ones that really get to you.

Do you ever suffer for your cause?

I was very allergic when I was younger and I was getting shots twice a week. A lot of the animal allergies I've grown out of, luckily. When I was working at the Zoo, I had an inhaler. Actually, it was kind of funny—when I was working with the elephants, the other keeper and myself were both allergic to hay. On Wednesdays, we'd get the hay delivered for the elephants and we had to unload 160 bales of hay from the truck. After, we'd both lie on the floor with our inhalers, going, 'Uuh uuh—can't breathe.' The rest of the time it was fine.

You're sometimes required to work up to 80 hours a week, which is unbelievable—a very stressful job. How do you maintain your stamina and your focus under conditions like that?

Some of the people close to me have a lot to do with that. My sisters hold me up at times. And other volunteers—some of the working board members are great. They're very supportive. Some of them recognize there are times—once in a while, things get so stressful—they say, 'Nathalie, get out, go home.' It's important. I consider most of the people on the working board to also be my friends. Well, we sort of have to be, because we work together so much, but they're great in that respect, because they know every once in a while they have to force me to get out—'Please go home and rest.' Because it does get really stressful sometimes, and you just have to keep thinking about why you're doing it and about the good that you're doing—and that it's going to get better in a few months. When it gets hectic—you know, the 80 hours a week that you mentioned—that's usually peak baby season, and that's something that ends. So you can say to yourself, 'Okay, the babies are going to grow older and this is going to end.' You have to stick it out. At least I can sleep now—in winter time. I hate winter, but at least I can rest a little bit.

Because yours is a young, non-profit organization, and you basically survive on donations, you haven't taken a salary yet. How do you pay your bills—how do you pay your rent?

Basically, the little bit of money that I do get, from gifts or tax returns or little things like that, I have to use to the utmost, every little penny. The first year on my tax return, I got almost $2,000 back, which is not much, but when you have no money coming in, it's a lot. I rely heavily on my family. My parents own the house that I'm in now, so I don't have to pay rent. I wish I could afford to pay rent, but I can't. My sisters and my friends support me a lot. My sisters—sometimes they'll say, 'Here, eat it. You haven't eaten all day.' I think just the support of a lot of people. It's very hard to survive with no income. I had savings initially, you know, that I'd put aside, but they've gone now and I do need to make a salary.

Do you ever take the time to celebrate or revel in your victories?

I don't think I've had time to yet. I'd love to go away with someone for a couple of weeks and have a vacation and just feel good about what's been accomplished to date, but I don't have the time or money to do that. Also, there's still so much pressure, so much more that needs to be done, that it's hard to relax enough at this point. I have to have people remind me, 'Look how much you've done. You've only been open for ten months.' Sometimes you can feel this overwhelming weight of everything else that still has to be done, but it's good to have people around to remind you.

I've learnt that for an animal to remain wild, they have to hate you. So when do you get the emotional satisfaction that we get from our pets?

There is a lot of satisfaction in other ways. Even if you can't hug them, they do hilarious things. They make you laugh. They do it when they think you're not watching. It makes your day better. A lot of the baby animals try to get affection from you. The baby raccoons will just be all over you when you're trying to feed them. So you get little bursts of affection from them when you're feeding. But you get a lot of satisfaction in letting them remain wild, because you know that they're going to live a normal life. After a while, it becomes a really happy thing when you think, 'This animal's going to be fine—because he hates people, and he's just going to run off into the forest and he knows how to do crayfishing and he knows how to socialize with his own.' You get satisfaction because you know you've done your job well and you're satisfied that he's going to live—and you can go on to the next little guy. I'm at the point now where, if an animal wants to be petted by people in the Wildlife Centre, it sort of depresses me. I think, 'Oh no, no. That animal's never going to make it out in the wild.' I growl at the animal and tell people to ignore it, big signs saying 'Ignore this animal, refuse its advances' sort of thing. We have to be really careful that doesn't happen with an animal because—what do you do with it?

Do you actually physically growl at them sometimes?

Uh huh. Everybody does. I make them do it.

Let's hear a growl.

GGGRRRR!!! It depends on the animal. Like, with raccoons, you have to be very forceful with them sometimes, even baby raccoons—growling and snarling and banging things. You have to make sure they will stay away from you, because raccoons more than anything want to become your pet when they're babies. They want to grab you and paw you, and you have to resist their advances because they're soooo cute. They really are. You always have to keep in mind their survival when they get released.

You've worked with elephants, with tigers and lions and I think rhinos?

I think I've worked with everything, by this time. Except maybe seals.

When does fear enter the picture?

When I'm put into a situation where it's an animal that I don't know, and I'm left there by myself, and I don't even know the personality of that individual animal, then sometimes I might be afraid. Or if the situation starts to get out of control and I don't how to control it. For example, once at the Zoo I was working with the elephants. I was cleaning one of the elephant pens and—the way elephants respect people is sort of on a hierarchy level. I was just a summer student and so I was below the full-time keepers, but I was above members of the public.

This is in the elephant's mind?

Yes, in the elephant's mind. They have this sort of respect they give to everybody that's there. They're very fine animals. I had gone into the pen and given them the command to move over to the side. I was cleaning in one area and there were three or four elephants in front of me. But one full-time keeper didn't know I was in the pen. So he came in to the front end of the enclosure and gave them all the order to back up. All of a sudden there are all these big elephant bums backing towards me in this corner. I was really scared there for a minute, because I thought I was going to be crushed by four eight-thousand-pound elephants. I was yelling to the keeper, 'I'm back here! I'm back here!' and the keeper gave them the command to drop down onto their stomachs and they all dropped—but they were only a few feet from me at that time. It was kind of scary.

You're in Mensa. Explain to me what that is.

I don't want to tell anybody I'm in Mensa. That was just something I sort of did for myself.

What is Mensa?

It's an academic club.

You have to have an especially high IQ, right?

You have to write two IQ tests to get into this club and then, if you get the cut-off level for the IQ, then they let you into the club.

From what I hear from people who know you, you have the ability to do whatever you set your mind to.

I think my parents probably had a lot to do with it. One thing that really stands out from my childhood—because there were three of us who were all girls—is that neither of our parents seemed to really acknowledge the fact that being female was anything different from being male. There wasn't any kind of gender bias when we were growing up. It was—you can do whatever you want. I know a lot of people are raised thinking, 'Well, maybe you could be a doctor or a lawyer or something,' but it's almost like that would be something that would be abnormal, because you were a girl. Like, if you were a really good girl, you could be a doctor or a lawyer. But it was—you can do whatever you want. My father would teach us to take apart motors, cut down trees, things like that. It was only—for myself in particular—when I was older and I started encountering people who hadn't been raised this way—like when I went to university and encountered some people who would best be known as chauvinist pigs—I didn't know people thought this way, you know? I had a motorcycle license which I got when I was 18, I guess. This one particular guy said, 'You have a motorcycle license? Girls can't ride motorcycles!' It was like he was speaking some foreign language—I thought, 'What are you talking about?' I realized that there were people out there who actually thought they shouldn't do something because they were female. Maybe in that respect it had a lot to do with my parents, because they were just—you can do whatever you want. And if we had an idea, that was really encouraged.

Would you consider yourself a feminist?

I've always had trouble understanding exactly why feminism seems to mean so many different things to different people. I guess I wouldn't like to be labeled a feminist. I'd rather be labeled as somebody who just believes in people—both genders equally. But if a feminist is someone who believes that women have as much ability as anyone on the planet to succeed, then I guess I am a feminist.

It seems that some people who call themselves feminists seem to be anti-men, which I think is ridiculous. They're just causing another problem in order to solve one problem. I think it's important for people to work towards equality, and that different people, whether they be men, women, whatever race, age, have different talents and different skills in different areas and we have to take everybody as an individual and respect them for who they are and the talents they have. Not necessarily just talents, but whatever aspects of their personality they have that are unique to them, you have to try to respect them for that. So I don't think women should be thought of as different in any way. They should just be people.

It's very physical, what you're doing at the Wildlife Centre. You mentioned that you built all the boxes for the animals, and when a bird comes through the door with a huge wing span, you physically have to hold it down. Are people surprised when they realize that you have to do

this kind of physical work and that you can manage it on your own?

Yes, they are, sometimes. I think—just getting back to the 'woman' thing again, I think maybe sometimes people are surprised when women don't have a problem doing physically challenging things. Sometimes I'll go into a store and buy something, and if there's a man there, sometimes he'll say—about a 20-pound bag of something—he'll insist that he carry it out to the car for me. 'No, no, you can't carry that yourself, you'll hurt yourself....'

Little lady.

And of course, I'm not going to turn around and say, 'Oh, don't you dare carry that for me,' because I know he's only trying to be polite. But at the same time, I'm thinking, 'I just carried a bag of feed that weighed three times that amount before I came here.' I have to watch at the Wildlife Centre, be more sensitive to people who are just starting out and maybe not used to doing this kind of physical work. I know the two co-op students we had—Jennifer and Jennifer—one of them finally said to me, 'We can't carry all this stuff.' And I had never even thought they would have trouble, because I just pick them up and carry them. And they said, 'You know, it's really heavy.' I said, 'Oh my God, I'm sorry, I didn't know. Just tell me if I ask you to carry something that's too heavy for you, because I didn't think about it.'

You're sitting across from me and I can see you're thin, but obviously strong. How did you get so strong?

I don't know—maybe it's something you get used to, carrying heavy things on a regular basis. I don't work out or anything, but I've always had jobs working with animals so I've always had to be lifting feed bags and bales of straw and hay. Sometimes it's hard to carry them, but I carry them anyway. Because they have to be carried.

That's sort of your philosophy of life—the bag has to be carried, so carry the bag. Are you aware that you set very high standards for yourself? I see that as a positive, but I assume that it would be intimidating for a lot of people.

I don't necessarily see it as a positive for myself. I don't think it's always a good thing for someone to always have these really high levels set for themselves to reach. Because you can't always reach them. If you set high levels for things you can't reach, then you end up always being disappointed about things.

You're a perfectionist.

Well, about some things. You cannot be a perfectionist about everything, it's impossible. You'd go absolutely mental. You have to reach a point with a lot of things that are good enough. But there are a lot of things, especially things that I feel are very important, that have to be exactly right. And that means it has to be exactly right coming from me. I can write out a letter and show it to six different people because I want it to be really good. I'll have all this input and I'll take it and make it even better. But just about specific things. My car is a mess.

Mine, too. I live in my car. How have you changed since your days at university?

I'm a lot more serious now, I think. Not because I want to be, just because I don't have the opportunity to do all the fun stuff that I was doing then—even though I want to. That's one of my goals, to get back to having time to spend with my friends and go to the cottage and things. But I think always having all this responsibility on me—literally seven days a week—definitely makes you a much more serious and subdued person. You can't go and get drunk and get hung-over and call in sick the next day. I can't let myself do it because who's going to go in? Some days if I plan it—if I have some specific reason that I want to have the next day off, I can plan it ahead of time. But I can't do anything impromptu, spontaneous, like I used to be able to do.

What's the best piece of advice that you've ever received?

There's something that I find myself saying quite a bit, and I don't know where it came from. But when I've been with people and we're trying to do something and we think, 'Oh, we can't do this,'

I've said to people several times, 'If we can put a man on the moon, we can find somebody to do this.' Like, there's got to be a way to do this. It makes sense to me.

When will you feel that you've succeeded?

When I can be well-rounded again. Before the Toronto Wildlife Centre, I had more time to spend with my friends and more time to go to the cottage—things that I want to get back to. But I wasn't as happy with what I was doing as an occupation. Now, assuming everything goes well at the Wildlife Centre—and I'm confident it will—I will have a job that I'm happy about and I'll feel I'm contributing something worthwhile, doing something worthwhile with my life. When I get to the point where I can balance spending time with my friends and family and actually having a life outside the Centre, I think that's when I'll be really happy with what I've achieved.

Sarah Polley

Sarah Polley's parents didn't want their daughter to have to deal with the stress of an acting career. After all, she was only three years old. But Sarah Polley has never let her age get in the way.

Before meeting Sarah, I had heard mention on several occasions of how grown up she was for her 15 years. So when we initially spoke on the phone, I was a little concerned and surprised when she suggested that we meet at the Granite Brewery for our interview. My fears of seeing Sara of Avonlea chugging back a few brews were quickly put to rest when I walked into what turned out to be a family restaurant and spotted this grunge-inspired teenager smiling at me.

Sarah Polley is a typical teenager, albeit a precocious one. She's just discovering the wonders and heartache of the opposite sex, some of her friends smoke pot and she worries about the environment. She has also been a professional actor since the age of four, and was recently named the most popular Canadian teenager on television, according to a poll conducted by *TV Guide*. Even though she's been working alongside actors three times her age for most of her life,

Sarah has managed to remain so, well, normal. Normal except for a noticeably developed vocabulary and a sophisticated way of articulating her numerous opinions.

Acting came naturally to Sarah. Born to parents who were both respected thespians, one could say performing was in her blood. She made her film debut at age four playing a waif in *One Magic Christmas*. By the time she was ten years old, she had won critical acclaim for her starring roles in the TV series, 'Ramona,' and the feature film, *The Adventures of Baron Munchausen*. For the past five years, Sarah has brought the character of Sara Stanley to life in the hugely successful television series, 'Road to Avonlea.' She's a veteran at 15 years old.

On the surface, Sarah's life seems to be right out of a fairy tale, although she's had her fair share of tough times. After her first season on 'Avonlea,' her mom was diagnosed with cancer. Sarah was ten years old when she lost her mom to the disease. But Sarah proved herself to be a true professional and, after a short break, threw herself back into work, even though it took all she had. It helped her deal with the loss. Considering the way she handled this difficult time in her life, her concentration and discipline must be remarkable.

It seems to me that Sarah has come to terms with being one of Canada's most famous young actresses. Instead of the glamorous lifestyle of a movie star, her daily routine is far more down to earth. She takes the art of acting very seriously, enjoying the process of researching her characters as much as performing them. She majors in drama and music at her high school, loves writing poetry, is counting the days until she can attend university and would ultimately like to start her own political party so she could make the world a better place. After spending an evening chatting with this idealist, I'd vote for her any day.

Imagine for a minute that you're Sarah Polley's agent and you're trying to get her the lead in a new dramatic series about teenagers. How would you describe Sarah the person?

Very focused. Not necessarily always focused on the same thing, but when she sets her mind to something, it's always in a very determined manner. Honest—sometimes to the point of being offensive, but always straight, or at least trying to be. Quirky, definitely quirky. I think I don't get into a lot of society's games—I don't play games with people. I'm always very focused and straight-ahead and very honest, nothing that can be interpreted any other way than it is. I'm not a die-hard feminist, but I do believe when you're a woman, to be honest is a much more shocking thing than when a man is.

How would your agent describe Sarah Polley the actress?

Subtle, low-key. Sometimes I think it can border on boring. I work so hard to be natural, because I see so much animated, over-the-top stuff—especially American sitcoms—that it forces me to the other extreme. What I don't always remember is that television and stage aren't your life, they're the illusion of life, and so sometimes it *has* to be pushed beyond the absolutely natural.

You grew up the youngest, by eight years, of five kids. Were there advantages to being the youngest?

Definitely. My brothers and sisters were going through high school when I was going through Grade 3 and 4, so they were always sort of teaching me and always wanting to spill all the knowledge and all the learning that they had onto somebody. Since I was younger and could be taught, I was the obvious choice. I definitely had an advantage from that standpoint and also, they'd always take me places. I was the little sister, especially with my brother, Mark, who thought it was really cool to have a little sister. We were always doing fun stuff together.

Do you still have the same relationship with your siblings, in that they continue to teach you?

Yes, most definitely. They've all gone through different things, but now they've all ended up back at university, except for one who's a counseling doctor. And they're all always teaching me what they learn and calling me on the phone discussing things. Because I can argue and debate more maturely, it's even better for them. Sometimes I skip off class to go to their lectures.

You go to the university lectures?

Sometimes, yeah. I skip school to go to the university—that's so stupid, but I do.

What kind of lectures do you attend?

I've been to one on modern English and one on Aristotle. It's really cool, because I really like reading, so it motivates me and gets me interested in new things. It spurs all kinds of new ideas in me.

Are you excited about going to university?

Very. Very. It's my dream—getting into Oxford. So all my focus right now is on getting to university.

Your dad is Michael Polley, an actor. And your mom, Diane, acted, and was a casting director. And your brother, Mark, was a child actor. In view of your family background, do you think that making your acting debut in *One Magic Christmas* at four years old was perfectly normal?

Because of my family, you mean? No, because I had to fight for it. I was only four, but my parents are both actors and my mom was in the business in other ways as well—my brother being a kid in acting—they knew it was hard. It's not that easy at all. It's really not an easy thing to go through, and they didn't want to subject me to it at all. They wanted me to lead a normal life and grow up normally, but I think I was pretty strong-willed.

How is a four-year-old strong-willed? How do you articulate to your parents what you want to do?

I think I just did. They had always taught us to be independent, to fight for what we wanted, and that's what I did. In this case it was against them, but they realized since I was about two that I just wanted to, wanted to, wanted to. Finally they realized that if I was going to make mature decisions, they had to let me make them.

At four years old.

Exactly.

How does a four-year-old audition? What do they look for?

I was actually reading for the lead role, which I didn't get because I didn't have any experience. At least, that's one of the reasons. I love actors who say, 'I didn't get it because of this and this and this and I had a cold too, so I didn't get the part.'

You could read at four years old?

Yeah—I learned to read, I think, probably because of my brothers and sisters. I started school early because I learned how to read very early.

If you had a four-year-old daughter who showed signs of being an actor, how seriously would you take her?

I don't know. I have a lot of philosophies about how to raise children. I probably believe in the way my parents brought me up. Although I don't think I could take her as seriously as my parents took me. I really respect my parents for that. It's a hard thing to do. I'm against age discrimination, but when it comes to a four-year-old, I don't think I could have had the trust they had in me. It's really amazing.

Explain 'I don't believe in age discrimination.'

Ahhh. A lot of things—it involves voting. I feel a lot of people under the age of 18 know more about the political parties that are running than people over 30. Everything from driving, from graduated licensing. I feel like people in my age group are really discriminated against.

Fifteen-year-olds.

Yes. And below that. I felt all my life I was really being oppressed. There were a lot of opportunities that I would have liked to have that were denied.

Can I play devil's advocate for a second and put forth the idea that perhaps you are far more sophisticated and mature than the average person your age?

Okay. This is the thing. I think that because I had educated parents and really educated brothers and sisters, I can express myself verbally quite well, comparatively. But I also feel that doesn't make me more sophisticated than my peers, because people, according to their upbringing, express themselves in different ways. In some ways, I'm a lot more immature than other people my age. All my friends have the same level of sophistication, it's just that I happen to have a way of expressing it that fits into society's way of judging who's smart and who's not.

You're very articulate. You also have some great ideas.

Do you know what, though? I think that anybody in Grade 10 at my school has ideas this big. But because I've been given the opportunity to work with adults all my life, people generally listen to what I have to say. A lot of people my age aren't given that respect, and I don't think they see the point in expressing themselves to older people because they don't think they're going to be listened to—and they probably won't be. It's all part of the discrimination. Adults don't listen to kids, then kids in turn won't express their ideas to adults—it's like a cycle.

You started at the School for the Arts at eight years old. What kind of subjects did or do you study?

At Claude Watson, the school that goes from Grade 4 to 8, we took dance three times a week, national dance, creative modern jazz, music three times a week, instrumental and vocal, drama twice a week and art twice a week.

So those were the subjects we studied at the same time as academics. The day was divided in half. Now I'm a drama major with an elective in music and also the academics.

What is it about acting that you love?

It's... it's... uh...

Interesting that this is a hard one for you to answer.

I know. It's because it's so hard to articulate. It's a way of understanding other people, I think, of putting yourself into positions, being different people, experiencing different emotions that you might not experience as yourself. I think it depends on the method you use, but mine is that I try and make myself that person in every way. Not to the point where it carries on into my daily life. It gives me a much better understanding of other people—where they're coming from. When I see someone acting like a complete jerk, I find that I have a tendency to be able to relate what I felt to what they're feeling. I feel it gives me an understanding of other people that I wouldn't otherwise have.

How do you develop a character?

It's changed as I've gotten older. When I was six, I didn't do a hell of a lot of research, but now—I'm doing *Through the Looking Glass* at Stratford this summer—I started reading *Alice*. And reading *Alice* leads to reading about Lewis Carroll, reading Lewis Carroll leads to reading about Oxford and reading about Oxford leads to—it leads to so much. You can be really overwhelmed or you can take it easy, do what you can. But right now, I'm just shoving myself full of stuff on Lewis Carroll. I've read about the drugs he was using at the time to inspire *Alice*—it's fascinating to go through all this research.

How does finding out about the drugs Lewis Carroll took help you to play the role of Alice?

I think, understanding what it was he actually saw. You research a drug like mushrooms or acid, and you feel through the books what that does to you and what effect it has on you, and how it makes you feel and what kinds of things come to you—and I think you get a clearer understanding of what he was seeing and what emotions he was experiencing when he thought of *Alice*.

Can you explain the process of what a day's shooting on 'Avonlea' involves?

You get to work. Usually, before we go through hair and makeup and wardrobe, we have a blocking. They light. We get into hair and makeup and wardrobe. You rehearse once or twice. And then we do it.

You rehearse only once or twice?

Yes—it's very—a lot of it is almost winged. It's so short, the rehearsal process. It's really interesting, because I don't know if that's done a lot on other series, but I guess it sort of is, because...

Television is fast.

Yes. And there are, obviously, negative effects, but I like the idea that when you're watching a television show, a lot of it happens at the moment. That adds a real aspect to it.

What about things like learning your lines? When they give you your script, how long do you have to learn your lines?

Well, we get a call sheet, which tells us the scenes we're doing the day after. So I usually look over it that night or in the morning when I get there, during the blocking. What I usually do is, when I get the script, I go through it a couple of times and make notes, and I get a real feel for how I'm going to play it. The lines are just, like secondary, you know. I don't have that much trouble learning lines. Occasionally I do, but lines are pretty easy.

What happens when you have trouble learning lines? How do you deal with it?

I actually almost had a breakdown. Second season of 'Avonlea.' This is so weird. I'm sure there was a lot of other stuff behind this, but there were a couple of scenes where I had speeches—big, whopping speeches—and I looked at them the night before as usual, and I was, 'OH MY GOD,' so I just—there were a couple of scenes where it would take four or five takes before I'd get it right, and I just freaked out because it had never happened to me before. It got to the point where, that whole year, before I'd do any scene, I'd feel nauseous. I was so nervous. I was a nervous wreck for a year. It was so odd.

You were 11 years old when this was happening?

Occasionally it happens again. I get a little glimpse of it and then I push it back down. It was a very weird feeling. I guess it has a lot to do with the age, too. I mean, until I was about ten, I didn't care what people thought. I was just having fun, doing what I wanted to do. Then all of a sudden, I started caring about what people were thinking.

Perhaps you were losing your innocence a little.

Yeah—maybe that's because I wasn't at a school that I could worry about, or if I was going out with somebody or if my hair and makeup was right. It came out in my career. All of a sudden I was worried about what people thought about my acting. I sort of realized I was on TV and that there was a crew there that would notice if I lost my lines.

What happens when you disagree with the director's vision? I would guess, sitting here talking to you after about six minutes, that you have a specific vision of who your character is. And the director has one. What happens when the two of you come to heads?

The thing is, we have a different director every episode. The actors basically have a pretty good idea of our characters after all this time. So they usually leave us alone. I think they respect that. Occasionally someone will give input, and that's totally cool and he does a good job. Sometimes people give input that I don't agree with. I'm not quiet for very long.

What I'm imagining is this sort of cute little girl dressed up in her frilly costume, pointing her finger at this director and going, 'Listen buddy, don't tell me what to do. I've been doing this for 11 years.' That's never happened?

No. Because I try to avoid power struggles and stuff like that.

Well you'd win. You're the star.

Well...I don't know about that either, but—I'm not really too keen on that kind of thing. If there's something that I really, really don't agree with and the director's not willing to budge on it, I take the direction and I try and find a way that it makes sense to me.

What's the best piece of advice you'd give to a director working with young talent?

This is assuming that all kids are like I am—to make the direction interesting, so that you will capture their attention. There have been times, when I was younger, that directors would repeat things and repeat things and repeat things—and I'd hear it, but I wouldn't be listening, so I wouldn't get it. Some directors say the same thing over and over and over again. They think because you're a kid, you'll forget. You have to make it interesting so you'll capture their attention.

What would your advice be to a young performer who has to work with a director?

To try and focus on what they're saying, and to really listen. And if you disagree, definitely do voice your opinion. But do listen. Because it affects the whole product.

What would you say makes a good actor?

Someone who never stops questioning. Themselves, the director, the show. Not to the point where you're completely self-conscious, but to the point where you don't have a set idea of anything and you're willing to smash down all your ideas about a character. That's what makes a good person, not just an actor, but a person.

In other words, someone who's always evolving.

Yes, definitely. Always willing to change, always willing to grow.

What is the glamorous side to your job?

Hmm. I guess being able to work with the people I work with. Being able to meet the people who I've met, and talk with them and learn from them. That's the most glamorous thing. I don't know what glamor means—if it's like having things done for you. I can't stand that. The one thing I really can't stand is when people open doors for you and help you down from places and go and get you things. It makes me crazy. I like to do stuff for myself and it feels like people are robbing me of my independence when that happens.

You're famous for bringing a famous Canadian literary character to life. How important is the 'Canadian' to you?

Not as important as the human being. I'm not a very nationalist person at all. I'm infinitely proud of what a peaceful nation this is, and the writers and the musicians and the actors and the dancers who have come out of this country, but I can't say I'm proud to be a Canadian, because I don't think that means anything. I'm more happy to be a citizen of the world.

In *TV Guide* there was a poll. You were voted the most popular Canadian teenager on television. Do you think they're picking you—or the character you play?

I think the character. I don't think that someone can really know me—there are aspects of me that are similar but—I think it has to be the character.

What is it about the character that you think they're drawn to?

I think because she's very sort of creative, and very dreamy and romantic, but at the same time very down-to-earth. She keeps her feet on the ground. And she has a huge conscience, for everybody. I think that appeals to people—someone with a good set of morals. It's something that people are hungry for in everyday life, so to see it on television is even better than the sex and the violence that usually get on there.

How different are you from your character?

I'm more extreme than her in a lot of ways. I take things too seriously sometimes, I guess. Once I get my mind set on something, I'm so extreme. Things like—well, about three months ago, I stopped wearing makeup and I became stupid about it. It was my decision. But I started imposing it on my friends, and I started saying stupid things like I wouldn't have as much respect for them if they continued to wear makeup. Once I get my mind set on something, it's very hard to pull me off. I've become obsessive about stuff like that.

Tell me why you chose not to wear it any more.

I guess there are a lot of reasons. But the main one is I found I was becoming a high-maintenance person. I used to put on a bit of mascara to go to school and then I started putting on a bit of foundation, lipstick, and it got to the point where I was putting on a lot of stuff and when I'd leave one of these things off, I'd feel gross. I'd feel ugly. I didn't feel like I was as good a person. I realized it was so much nicer to get to the point—get out of bed, whip on whatever was in the closet and go to school and concentrate on what I was doing, rather than how I was appearing.

I'm surprised that you even wore makeup. Firstly, because you're absolutely beautiful. And second of all, it's part of your job to wear makeup on set, so one would think that you would relish the hours where you're makeup-free.

I know. I can totally see that being true, but a lot of it is being 15. I don't know whose approval we're looking for, but we're looking for someone's approval. It seems like my whole life, all my friends, anyone around me my age, we're all struggling for somebody's approval. Some macho idiot in the hall whistling or anything. It seems like there's a lack of encouragement or enthusiasm about us.... All my friends are stressed out about school, about how they look, about everything imaginable and about making their family happy—I don't know if my sisters and brothers ever were—it feels like it's gone from an extreme to an extreme. Like, in the '60s and '70s and even the '80s, it seemed like everyone was very rebellious and everyone was sort of trying not to please everyone. Now it seems that everyone in my grade is trying to please everyone and it's gotten to the point where it's stupid.

Do you have people recognizing you wherever you go?

I used to—a lot. But I cut my hair in the summer. Since then, I've had about two people come up to me. It's the best thing I've ever done. Now nobody recognizes me, hardly at all, except actually these posters that just went up on the subway for 'Avonlea.' I take the subway to and from school, and I always seem to end up underneath one of them. I notice people are looking at me and I'm just, like, oh God—and I look up and there's my face, on the subway—it's so embarrassing. It looks like I've planted myself right under my picture. It's bad.

Why do you think there is such a fascination with famous people?

That's a very hefty question. I definitely can't answer that 100 per cent. I can say, though, that it probably has something to do with the fact that you have the power to enter anyone's home by them just pushing a button. You can enter their lives, you can grab their attention for an hour, you can get into their houses and take up their time.

How would you make sure that you're unaffected by your fame?

Above all else, that you always have a strong love for yourself. If you truly love yourself, what other people think, whether it be good or bad, won't matter that much to you.

When did you figure this out?

You know what? This is a culmination of a lot of things I've been thinking. This is the first time I've articulated it.

This always happens, though, when people ask me questions. Thoughts occur to me, but they're never really put into ideas until someone asks me about it. Things have been happening my whole life to help me form that opinion. Now that I have the chance to articulate it, it just comes together naturally.

Your agent was quoted as saying, 'I negotiate her fees, but I also negotiate her lifestyle.' What does that mean?

It means that when you're an agent of a kid—the time that I have to work affects my whole life, because it affects whether I go to school a lot, whether I see my friends a lot, how much time I get to spend with my family. I'm working towards my priorities in life, my real, true goals, which don't actually lie in acting. It's my friends and my social life and learning how to relate to people. So by negotiating my contract, she negotiates a lot of things in my life.

Have you ever turned down a role?

Yes. Always because of school. I've had to and I still have to make a lot of decisions. I've gotten to the point in acting where I think I'm eligible for quite a bit of work. I've never seen myself as an actor when I'm older, so I have to decide whether I'm going to sacrifice my education, which might lead to that goal sooner, or let it wait a while. I have to do a lot of thinking in the next little while.

Are you ultimately in charge of your career?

Yes, 100 per cent. I don't have anyone telling me what to do. My dad is going to let me do exactly what I want. He's 100 per cent in support of every decision I make. Every decision I make now—I'm 15—is going to affect me for the rest of my life. Whether it be in acting or my education.

You have pressure.

It is a lot of pressure. It would almost be easier if I did have someone telling me what to do, but I've been given that kind of independence and freedom of choice. My agent doesn't tell me what to do. She's like my friend. If I don't want to work, she doesn't say anything about it. My dad wants me to do what I want. I have to do all this on my own. It's hard.

So what do you base your decisions on?

That's what I have to figure out, too—long-term or short-term. In the past, it's been long-term, because I've always favored education over acting. But now I'm starting to think more short-term. I don't know if it's going to last—but there have been a couple of ideas flying through my head. Like opportunities to audition for certain things, to do certain things—seize the day.

So, in essence, if you were to get these roles that you would audition for, you couldn't go to school?

Right. I'd do it by a tutor. I'd still get the same quality of education, and it's great learning one-on-one, but I wouldn't have the social life. I'd really miss my friends. I have amazing friends. And it's a different experience learning in a classroom. It's being involved with other students—with your peers and with teachers. So I don't know if that's an experience I really want to miss. Also that could really help my chance of getting into Oxford, having a degree like an arts degree from Earl Haig, which is an amazing school. Dunno. I've got to think about that. I'm being so heavy.

You are heavy. You're serious. But you've been working since you were four years old. Wouldn't that force you to be a serious person?

I don't remember being serious. I think it's just in the last year I've become a really intense person. I've just been, like, so—contemplative and heavy about everything. I don't remember—in my life—always being like this. I don't know what it is.

For me, that's a good time—to get heavy. I like that.

Okay, good. It seems like you've come to the right person.

Is there a spiritual side to your life?

No, I don't think so. No. I think there was a time, probably close to when my mom died, that I became very stringent. I read a lot about Buddhism and I became very sort of Zen. I became very involved with things like crystals—actually very involved with crystals, and supernatural powers and...

You were 11 years old when that happened?

Yeah. A lot of that for me—and I'm not saying it's true for everyone who's a Zen Buddhist or believes in crystals—but for me, it was looking for something to grasp on to, something to believe in, something to keep me going. But I realized...I think I got past it. It was a phase I went through. I'm very atheist. Which might have a lot to do with my upbringing. I can't deny that at all. Because maybe if I had had someone reinforcing all the ideas of Zen Buddhism, I might still be a Buddhist. Maybe that's not the right way to deal with spirituality, but I don't have faith in anything but my fellow human beings and the world around me. I have strong faith in people, but not beyond people. The world is a beautiful place, it's a beautiful enough place for me to worship and have faith in and—it's enough for me.

So when times get tough now, in your day-to-day life, where do you get the strength to keep on going?

In the fact that I've got one life to live, even though it's just a glimmer of consciousness in, like, an ocean of consciousness, and in time that goes on forever beyond human beings. Even though I just have one life to live and it might mean nothing in the long run, all the more reason to enjoy it, because I have nothing to lose. I have absolutely nothing to lose. I have only experience and knowledge and fun and everything to gain. I have no one who's going to tell me I've sinned when I die, so—I'm having so much fun.

When something bad happens—say if someone bashed into your car, how would you handle it?

Well, that's life. Maybe tomorrow something wonderful is going to happen.

You lost your mom when you were 11—to cancer—so who became the female role model in your life?

Actually, that was a weird situation. Because—I'm sure this happens in a lot of girls' lives who lose their mom—you have about ten people trying to be your mom and trying to take her place and trying to give you that. It's completely not a selfish thing in most cases. I had a lot of women who wanted to fill that role. Some of them realized, on their own, what they were doing and backed off. But the fact was, and the fact still is, that I don't have a mother. It's something I have to live with. That's what I realized, too, because I was clinging to people, even on set...and I would become really close to them. But...my mother died. I have a father. My experience is very different from most people's. Most people grow up with a mother and a father. I'm growing up with a father. It's different, but I don't think that I'm missing out on having a mother, I'm gaining the experience of having a father. Obviously I'd rather my mother was still alive, but it's not something that you can ever replace and it's not something that I think you should want to, because it's the course your life takes and to look for something else is destructive.

Let's say that there are a lot of women in my life now who are really important to me. A lot of them are my age, some of them are older. I've taken—I guess I've had a really cool experience because

I've sort of created my own mother for myself. I've taken all the best qualities from all my friends who are women and tried to emulate those.

What's the best piece of advice that's helped you through the tough times?

It's going to sound really strange. The more I hear it, the more it makes sense to me, 'Nothing really matters.' It sounds like a bad thing. But it's gotten me out of the worst depressions and the worst frames of mind ever.

But explain why nothing really matters?

Someone said this to me—it's like a baby scratching its knee. At the time, it's a huge deal to this baby—it's screaming its head off, it's never felt so angry in its life. When it's 20 or even ten years old, is it even going to remember it? No. This could be the worst thing that's ever happened to us in our life, but if what makes us happy is caring about the world and the grand scheme of things, what does this really matter in the huge picture? We're probably going to look back on it and smile and say, 'Oh well, that was sort of sad, but look where I am now because of it.' It doesn't matter all that much. It couldn't matter as much as we think it does.

So what you're learning is perspective.

Yes, to have a perspective on things.

Times will get tough and then times will get good, and ultimately, in the bigger scheme of things, don't waste your time on this little problem because there are big ones coming up.

Exactly.

I read that you've incorporated the pain of loss into your character. That's a very sophisticated acting technique. And also a very sophisticated coping technique.

You know what, though? I hate to tell you this. I don't do that any more. I've actually realized it is one of—in my opinion—the biggest mistakes anyone can make. The biggest, most destructive thing someone can do. I used to use it for all my crying scenes, my mom dying. After a while, when I would think about her and start crying, I would feel the worst guilt—I don't think I've ever told anyone this before but, well...the worst guilt that you can imagine because it was like—I use this for my acting, I use it for my job. All of a sudden, all the emotion, the real emotion that I could feel about this, seemed artificial. It seemed so contrived, because this was what I was doing to make a scene easier to play. I don't believe in that method of acting any more. I completely changed all my principles, because relating your own personal experience is destructive, not only to yourself but to the whole product. Even though that character lost her mother and I lost my mother, although those events are similar, they come from completely different backgrounds. They are two completely different people, as people always are—so for her to deal with her mother's death in the same way that I'm dealing with my mother's death isn't true to the character at all. It doesn't work for the character—it's destructive for me—it's not worth that. No job is worth that.

So now, in those scenes when you have to cry, how do you do it? Onions?

Hmmm. What do I do? I try and be in the character and be in the moment and be the character for that moment. It's a lot more fair to the audience and it's a lot more true to yourself.

If your mom knew that it was her loss that brought tears to your eyes as an actress, do you think that it would have bothered her?

Maybe. I don't know. She died when I was 11, and she was sick for two years before that, so I don't know how well I knew her. I knew her as my mom, she was a great mom, but my brothers and sisters had got to a point where they knew her on a more personal level because they were at an age where they could really talk to each other.

It's true that, as we grow up—and it happened to me, too—you see them as mommy and daddy and then one day,

you go, 'Hey, my daddy's a really good-looking man.' Or, 'My mom, she's an interesting person.'

Yeah—all of a sudden they're real people to you.

You never really got that far with your mom because you weren't old enough.

I have sort of glimpses of it—I have vague memories of it. It's hard, you know. She had five kids. And she had a job. And she really gave me a lot.

Was she a feminist? Your mom?

Hmm. I don't know. I know that she was for women's rights 100 per cent. But I don't know if I could call her a feminist.

What's your definition of feminism?

I've never actually thought about it before but, strangely enough, as liberated as I think I am, I think I associate negative things with that. Isn't that weird? I find that really, really weird.

What do you associate it with?

Angry. A lot of anger. I guess that's awful, and I've never even noticed that before. But I do associate a lot of anger with feminism and with people who call themselves feminists and I know that's wrong.

But you called yourself a feminist at the beginning of this interview.

Oh—I said I'm not a diehard feminist. I believe in equal rights for men and women. I don't believe in the coming about of that equality by—I know that a lot of feminists—from what I've heard in interviews and things and from what I know—have said.... Yes, I agree that men and women should be equal, because right now we don't have as great a status as men. We have to push for superiority just to get equality. We have to shoot to the top just to get half way. I can definitely see that point. But I think it's very dangerous to start shooting for superiority instead of equality, even though you might not get as far as fast. It becomes—it doesn't become the goal of equality any more.

So in a sense, you're a liberated woman—you're in charge of your financial side, you're in charge of your career,

you're allowed to make your own decisions. Maybe you're the ultimate in what the feminist movement is striving for. You're the living embodiment of what these women have been fighting for for so many years.

Well, you definitely have a point. Because obviously, if feminism hadn't been around I wouldn't have the opportunities I have now. So, yes, I think it's very wrong of me to associate anger with feminism. But it's a lot of stereotyping media that's contributed to this, and a lot of scared men who have contributed to my viewpoint of what a feminist is. The media is run by upper-class males, so obviously, I'm going to have the image, living in the society that I do, that feminists are this group of people we should be afraid of.

One of the things I heard about you before I came here was that you're very interested in politics. To the point of even considering one day, maybe, starting your own political party. A lot of young people mistrust politicians. Why do you want to become one?

Maybe one of the reasons this generation has such a low sense of morale is that we have no trust in the people who are leading us, who are making all the decisions for us and the way our lives are run. It would be great to be a leader the people could trust. Someone who's actually honest. Because I am honest, that's one thing I can say about myself. I'm very focused on what I believe and I have strong beliefs. And I definitely question them and I do change them often, but there are things that I don't think I will ever agree with.

So you do want to get into politics. What do you think defines a good leader?

Someone who gives people confidence in themselves and in each other. Not nationalism—not confidence that they are a great country and the greatest country and that because they're Canadians, they're superior to everyone else—but a confidence in themselves as people and as individuals. I would never ever want to intrude on anybody's rights, like they did in the Soviet Union, because that's what destroyed it. As individuals, as a culture, as a whole race of human beings. Trust. I think people need to have trust in a leader. For a change that extreme, I think people need to have a huge amount of trust in their leader.

It happened to Ronald Reagan—here is this actor from America, becoming the president. You have a very down-to-earth, charming persona—who knows? In 30 years, we could have Prime Minister Polley.

Yeah, well, I hope I don't end up like Ronald Reagan.

Would you like to be prime minister?

I don't know. Until a couple of months ago, I used to say I wanted to be the prime minister—that's all I wanted. To go to Oxford and then be the prime minister. Now I don't know. I'm watching the documentaries on Trudeau. He was very lucky because he didn't have to lie. He was in the right place at the right time. He was smart, he was honest. He is, I think, the coolest prime minister that any country could ever have. He is so cool. But he was lucky, you know. Most people have to lie their way to the top. From what I can see, it's very difficult to do it honestly. So I don't know if I can deal with that. I don't want to lie. If I can do it honestly, yes, definitely I will. If I can't, I won't. I'll be a poet. I want to be a poet anyway.

A poet or prime minister.

A poetician.

As a young actor, is there any one role you'd like to play when you get older?

Ummm. Antigone. She's a character in a Greek tragedy. She's the most strong-willed, indomitable, fiery, honest person. She's so cool. You should read that—you'd like it a lot.

Are you at all like this character?

I try to be like her in a lot of ways. She really lived, you know. So I'd like to think of myself like her. I've had it pretty easy, but I believe there are no limits anywhere. No one's ever put limitations on me, but I've seen people overcome things that they didn't think were possible. That's how I would want to influence people, letting them know there are no limits and there are no bars too strong to break.

What do you hope people learn from this interview?

I think that people have a large lack of trust in people of my generation. They feel that we don't have any goals. And we don't really feel we're going anywhere. I get that impression. I hope that I come across as someone who has a lot of goals and a lot of dreams and is focused and willing to do anything to achieve them. And I hope that gives people a bit of hope for the future. That there's someone who cares, a lot of people who care.

And you say you're willing to do anything to achieve your goals?

Everything except lie—except be dishonest. Yes.

Susan Aglukark

Pinning Susan Aglukark down for this interview was one of the most difficult tasks I was faced with while putting this book together. Media interest in Susan, both as a songwriter and as spokesperson for the Inuit people, is becoming so great that even before her debut album on EMI has been recorded, she is gracing magazine covers, touring non-stop and winning awards.

It's hard to believe that all of this attention has been based solely on the release of her low-budget, independent cassette, *Arctic Rose*. As a matter of fact, the only reason I had the good fortune to spend an afternoon with Susan in the first place was because the CBC had flown her in from Ottawa to pick up a very prestigious award for developing Native culture. Needless to say, things are happening quickly for her.

Susan Aglukark was born 26 years ago in the small, isolated community of Arviat on the west coast of Hudson Bay. The middle of seven children, she had a typical upbringing in the Arctic, except for the added pressure of being the daughter of the town's Pentecostal minister. Her father's way of life had a major impact on her development. He instilled in Susan remarkable strength and deep religious beliefs. Watching him preach his sermons fired up her passion for performing, but for an Inuit teenager living so far north, the possibility of actually making it as a professional performer was never more than a dream.

Obviously, the dream is coming true, but the route there has been hard and emotionally devastating. Life changed for Susan at nine years of age when she was sexually abused. After years of living with her painful secret, 19-year-old Susan decided to do something about it by going public and charging the man. A long and difficult court battle ensued, and when it finally ended, Susan knew she had to go as far away as possible from the scene of the nightmare. So she headed south to Ottawa and found a job with the government translating Inuktituk. It was there that her dream of becoming a singer/songwriter started to become a reality. After a series of fortuitous events, Susan began spending more and more time writing, singing and recording. She eventually gave up her day job and threw herself into performing full-time.

Susan's love of the north, her community and their difficult lives became the subject of her songs. Suddenly a group of people with precious few role models or leaders was discovering a young woman who was singing for and about them. Her songs are almost always written and performed in her native tongue, celebrating her heritage and the northern Canadian way of life. Without realizing the huge job ahead of her, Susan took on the responsibility of becoming a role model for all the young people growing up in the north, in the hopes of lessening their increasing sense of alienation. She also continues to be very outspoken about sexual abuse, spending any free time traveling around the small northern communities, counseling young people about this serious problem.

Susan is handling all this responsibility with grace, and her efforts aren't going unrecognized. She was chosen one of the "100 Leaders to Watch For" in *Maclean's* magazine and was named the 1993 Northerner of the Year in the Northwest Territories publication *Up Here*. Still, Susan's feet are firmly planted on the frozen ground. She is aware that her debut album, which is scheduled for release in 1994 has the potential to introduce the entire world to her culture. With Susan Aglukark's strength and conviction, this daughter of a preacher hopes to spread her music and, through it, make it possible for many other Inuit kids' dreams to become a reality like hers have.

Can I just say something? I think it's so great at your age to be wanting to write a book like this. I haven't met many people who are in our age group who actually think that big—enough to want to share it with the rest of the world.

You do.

Yes—I guess that's why a lot of the time when I was growing up in a small town—you can't discuss these kinds of things with people, because nobody can understand. Which is why I didn't.

If you didn't have any role models, how did you know you were missing one?

I realize now that what I was starving for, craving for, was an understanding of what I wanted to be as an artist. Or as a person as a whole, because I feel I've always been this but never had a chance to explore it. I could never really discuss it with my sisters and brothers, and there's nobody in a small town who would understand it. Even then, I couldn't go to the local library, which really was non-existent at the time, and look for say, Alan Morris, John Clavell, or other aboriginal role models. I didn't know they existed. And if I did, I wouldn't have been able to reach them anyway. To even think of somebody whose path I could follow—I just couldn't do it.

There's a very strong emphasis on elders and tradition in the North. So one would think that there would be strong role models.

The tradition is based more on respect for elders, but their life was not designed to create. The elders lived their lives day by day, to survive. Elders had the wisdom and the knowledge they had gained and hoped to pass that down. Their basic instinct has always been to survive a day at a time. Not next year, not in ten years, but let's just concentrate on today and see what happens.

And so for kids with big dreams, that's hard.

I've always daydreamed or imagined—two different ways of dreaming. One was, you can watch TV, and you see somebody you want to be like and you know in a small town it's impossible. So you only allow yourself to dream so much. You can only be part of that world to a certain degree and then after that, you cut it off. Then there's the other way, where you're so determined to be that person, to do what you want to do, that it doesn't end there. You go beyond. Mine was, I ended it there. For a long time. Even up until I moved to Ottawa five years ago in August, I had no idea that I could do this. I had no intention of getting this far with my music or my singing. In a way, that's what happens in small towns with young people. It's so limited because there are no role models. There are no people to actually pave the way.

You chose to leave your small town to move to Ottawa, where dreams became more possible. You were closer to a record company, people saw you.

But the intention when I left was not my music. When I left Rankin and Inuvik, I had spent a month there for my court hearings. I left to get away from them. To get away for a break, and it was just for a year. The August that I left was my first live performance ever, and it was just for fun. I'd never done anything before and didn't think I'd do anything after. It was just one of those fun things, because the guys played guitar and we got together and played guitar and sang the songs and it was fun—driving into Ottawa, the big city—that was it. I didn't know that I'd get involved with the CBC radio program, or the videos—it just happened.

What I think is interesting, though, about this story is that you did it. You didn't do it with any big hopes or dreams. An opportunity arises, a small opportunity, and you take it and you do it. And sometimes things come from it and sometimes they don't.

A lot of my decision-making has been based on 'it's too late to turn back now,' because most of the young people back home know me as a singer now, they hear me all over the place, and to back out now would be like—oh, another one of those leaders who could have been but didn't happen. I didn't want that to happen because I have to put myself in their shoes and I have to say I know what it would be like to be so disappointed. So I decided, 'Let's go one step at a time.'

You dreamt about it, but you never consciously thought that you could do it.

Which is why I have to explain, in my own mind, in a small-town girl's mind or a small-town kid's—there's only two ways of dreaming. One, you can only go so far; two, if you want to, you have to work ten times harder. I haven't done either. I've been very lucky. I'd allowed myself to imagine. Sitting at home, watching TV—God it would be nice to get a Juno, it would be nice to...even to just sit there and watch the artists.

Are you going to the Junos this year?

Yes, I think so.

What are you wearing?

I haven't decided yet.

Would you wear an Inuit outfit?

I'd like to. I've done a lot of modeling with fur and for a while I decided I'd stay away from that because I wasn't ready for...

The backlash. The politically correct backlash.

Sure. I thought about it and a lot of people called and said, 'We're not going to push you, but we need you to do this if you want to do it.' And if it helped people back home, I thought, 'Okay.' I did my first photo shoot with fur coats and they offered me one. I had to turn it down, because I don't want a fur coat. But I was staying away from that because of what I figured might happen, but then I thought, 'Why? It was never the Inuit way to go out there and hunt for the fur—we use every piece of the animal that we can.'

If they could spend a day or two with someone like my mother and my dad and my brothers and me, and watch them hunt, watch them skin the animals and what they do with the meat. Take the skin to my mom, who cleans it. And the hours she spends cleaning it. The days, the weeks, the months it takes to dry it the way you need it to sew it into whatever it is she's going to make up. I have two pairs of mukluks at home—footwear that she made. They have winter clothing that my dad needs for caribou hunting. If people could watch it, they'd realize that.

You've been described as a preacher's kid. How would your dad, the preacher, describe you?

The perfect preacher's kid. That's honestly how I was. And I grew up alone because of it. I think it's safe to say that out of seven children in my mom and dad's family, I'm the only one totally committed to Christianity. Because of my experience when I was a child, I needed something—even at that time, as a child, it was not as real to me as it is now—that is, God. I needed something to hold on to. That was real. That made me feel I was a normal person and didn't deserve what happened. That is what made me feel whole and pure. I grew up in the church. I decided at a very young age to help, to take away the mental anguish, because I was experiencing it myself. I found a lot of peace in myself in the church, and I spent a lot of time in there. I guess I would be the perfect preacher's kid, if they gave you the criteria of what a perfect preacher's kid would be like.

Which is what?

I was never on the streets. If I was, I was with friends. I'd bring kids home. I'd actually get the Department of Social Services on mom and dad's back because I was helping kids all the time.

What's your best memory of growing up, a middle child, with five girls and two boys?

Today, my brothers are both with me in Ottawa. I never really felt like a sister. I never felt like a girl. My best memories have always been as a tomboy and being able to—even if they didn't like it, beat them. If I didn't beat them, I'd challenge them. What was nice about it was that my older brother would let me have that space. It was fun. It's strange, but I don't ever feel...feminine. Strange, but I do and I don't. But I'm not in a totally confused state about it. I like it. I like being in control.

I'm the same way. I always say act more like a guy than a girl. But that's assuming that the traditional definition of a woman is passive, traditional, a homemaker.

Exactly the way it is for Inuit. I don't want to be that. I just turned 27 yesterday and it's like—my sister, who's 11 months older than I am, has been married for nine years, has two boys, and she's only 11 months older. To compare our age differences, and traditionally and historically with the Inuit, I should have been married ten years ago and have four or five kids. I'm not even in a relationship—and I love it. That's the way things are becoming for the Inuit people. But my mom and dad—not so much my mom, now that she understands what kind of person I am and that she can't make me do things like she used to. She realizes now that I'm my own person and she can't expect me to be like my sisters. Things change in cultures, and this is one of them.

Is the definition of success for women, in the Inuit culture, to get married and bear many children?

Success is not a big thing in the Inuit culture. Just to help other people to survive day by day. There were those who could hunt better and because of that they made them leaders. Maybe that was success. I'm not sure. But we'd have to get down and define success based on the culture.

Maybe the term should be 'generate pride.' A mother or father would be proud of their daughter if she was married and had many children.

I think so. That's the best thing. Even now, we had this incident back home, over the holidays. My family got all excited that somebody was actually interested in me and I had a chance at settling down. But for me, it's not what I want to do. But for them, it would be a perfect world if I did. I wasn't upset—I understood. That is the way among the Inuit people. That is how they'd feel proud of me.

What shape would you say that feminism takes in the northwest? I know that the women have to do the bulk of the domestic work, so to speak. Is feminism an issue there?

I don't think it is. Again, because there are so many changes going on. If you look at the political scene right now, the majority of the politicians are female—the ones that are in the higher positions. Twenty years ago they were all men. Twenty years ago it was okay for the woman to stay home while the man went traveling. Because of the changes that are going on—honestly, if I could use myself as an example, when I think about it—if I had the chance, I would marry an Inuit because I love my food, I love the way it's prepared, I love hunting, I love being able to sew for my husband, I love being able to do all that stuff and just be there for him. But if I married an Inuit, he would never accept my position—my lifestyle—it would be the most impossible thing for him to do. And I wouldn't want to put him through that. So I have to make that compromise when I get into a relationship. Honestly, I don't think I'm going to find anyone who could accept this kind of position, this status. I've had to accept the fact that this is going to go higher. Where I am right now is not where it's stopping. I won't allow it to. Not because I want to get up there, but because that's where it's going.

And you're the boss.

Exactly. Of my life and my career. I'm just learning that and I'm loving it. But it depends on a lot of things. Because tradition and culture—a lot of it stays the same, but just as much changes. I don't know if it would depend on the population of males and females in the Inuit culture, because there are more Inuit women than there are men, and if that's the case, then there will be more Inuit women in higher positions, and if that's the case, it will affect the whole system.

I'm reading a book right now. It says that in an igloo—in a home—if a man was known as the best hunter, he'd be known because of his wife—because the wife put him there.

Well, that's true. Behind every great man is a great woman. You mentioned an igloo. I understand you've never been in one.

Aside from five minutes I spent doing an interview. Igloos now are mostly built for competition.

People don't live in them any more?

They could. They still do over the Christmas holidays, usually when men go hunting. Part of the traditional feast is caribou. A lot of men go hunting and often a blizzard will come up, as happened this Christmas. If they can't come home, they'll build an igloo. So igloos are still used today, but not as often as before.

What kind of businesswoman are you?

Do we have to discuss this? Ha ha. A lot of my decision-making is based on the 35,000 people I represent. Unfortunately, many of my decisions are based on that. I know my limitations. I'll know if I can deliver or not, and if I can't, I'll say no, and I won't play around. If I feel any reason, or hesitate for any reason—if my insecurity comes in the way of my decision, I have to put my people ahead of that. If I feel I can deliver and personally I'm afraid I might not be able to, I'll take my chance and try, because I'm really the only one of 35,000 people who is at this level. I can't say no to something that might affect them in a real and bigger way. So my window, or view, is based on that vast part of Canada that nobody ever really thinks about—people that are Inuit. It's a part of business and a part of decision-making that a lot of people might not ever think about—or that path they might never take when they have to make decisions about business.

Do you think part of your success can be attributed to your unique heritage?

On a professional level, I think it is. In the environment of the world of arts and entertainment, it's because of my culture, it's because of what I could bring in. It's because of the colors and the different looks and different sounds that could be part of my music. On a personal level, when I meet with my manager, my management company, I know it's because of what I have. That's what they have helped me to realize. I was very insecure in the beginning. I didn't want to get into this just because I'm another average artist who can make it big because the rest of Canada needs a change. I didn't want to do that. I fought, and I'm still fighting, for people to recognize me as an artist first of all, and then as an Inuit artist.

The song 'Searching,' which is your biggest hit yet—what's it about?

The title is very general, when you speak about searching, because the song talks about searching in so many different areas of our lives. The song was written about a friend of mine who committed suicide. His entire life represented, unfortunately, what happens to most young people who go away to high school in the north. When you leave home at 15 or 16, there is a certain sense of excitement—it's a different place, it's a whole group of different people, it's a whole new set of emotions you're going to experience. Unfortunately, because of the traditional values that are very different growing up in a small town and in an Inuit family, compared to the values that you are suddenly plunged into in a residential school or in a residence where you're staying, everything changes. That, coupled with being 15 or 16—your most critical emotional growing time—all of that put together is a big change. But people make it. They have to, to get an education, but lots of people don't. What that forces a young person to do, if they decide to, is to search. It's an inner search. It's a search for strengths. What you think you have, what you can have and where you can find them. For a lot of young people, they think the answer is in drugs or alcohol and unfortunately it happens to plenty of people. But a lot of them can break away and find a better person within themselves.

There are so many different avenues to go, so many ways to search or not search. That's what the song is all about. It can be so many different fields of flowers. Unfortunately, this friend of mine—he could have... We were going out and he was the perfect Inuit male. He did everything that an Inuit man could do, and he had the brains for education, and he wanted to get into law. He wanted to do so much.

He was six foot three inches, so he played basketball and volleyball. He could do anything he wanted to do. But he killed himself at 17—a month out of high school. He could go to college—he could do anything—and, just like that....

It seems to me that you have to be very strong, always, in dealing with a lot of expectations. You've been called an ambassador for the Inuit and a woman of wisdom. Your record company describes you as a spokesperson for your whole culture. That's an awful lot of pressure.

I guess this is where I have to give credit to my mom and dad for their standing firmly for what they believe, which is their faith. They brought us up in what they believe, and what I grew up watching and learning from them is not necessarily the relationship they have with God, but what they believe in. They believe so strongly in it that no cultural upheaval, no changes, no nothing in the Inuit tradition could change their minds. No problems that we've experienced in our family—and there have been a lot—could change their minds.

When I'm performing in the North, automatically what happens is that at the end of the songs, you also end up with a counseling session. You end up on the phone with a family who needs a great deal of help. That is the only time when I have a very difficult time. Because it always happens, no matter where we go in the north. It will always happen and it's something I have to accept in my career. Even when I'm at home, we'll get long-distance calls from parents, or a couple who needs marriage counseling. And it all goes back to the wife being abused as a child. It always happens. So you get these phone calls and—that will always affect my personal life. That's the only time it gets difficult, because you get so emotionally drained.

You were the unfortunate victim of sexual abuse when you were nine years old. But it seems to have been a catalyst for change in your life.

It doesn't run my life. I don't want it to be what has made my career. I don't want my career to be based on an incident. It will be a part of me all my life, but it affects him as much as it affects me every time I speak about it. Him and his family. Every time I go home, he's there. So I don't want it to be there all the time. It will be. But there are ways to avoid it, somehow. I'm avoiding making it what I am today or letting it be what I base my career on, because it's not.

I think it took a lot of courage to stand up and identify the man who abused you.

This is a great big circle now. My older brother favors me. Of all the brothers and sisters, I've always been his favorite—or his punching bag. He married into that family without knowing, because the only people who knew were my parents. He married into the very family that abused me. His wife—they're now separated, not because of the incident—but his wife had a child before she married my brother and unfortunately, we've learned that after they got married, the same person that abused me, abused that child. And that was 12 years later. But what I had to think about when I first moved to that community—when I finally moved back after about 12, 13 years—was, if what he did to me 13 years ago is still going on today and he's been doing it for 13 years, how many other victims are up there? And my step-niece, when I think about it, she was only seven years old. My decision was, I had to do it. It was my statement that got him his sentence. The two other victims were too young and I guess the court thought their statements wouldn't stand up in trial, so it was my statement that got him a year and a half.

Only a year and a half!

That's how it happened for me. And I am glad that it happened. It forced me to realize I had a lot of potential that I wasn't using, that I wasn't looking into, because of what happened. It opened a lot of—it broke a lot of mirrors, I guess. It made me realize there was another person behind the mirror. I go beyond what I see in front of it. There are still a lot of issues that I'm dealing with because of that. But it did force me to accept the fact that I am a lot better than I thought I was.

And that you can actually effect change. You personally changed the route of this man's life.

His life, his family's life and the lives of a lot of other victims and abusers. So I guess it did help a lot.

As a spokesperson for your people and your culture, what is the message?

The biggest message is a simple one, because I've experienced it and am experiencing it. And that's—you can be what you want to be. Which I guess basically is saying—there is so much more within us than we realize. Unfortunately, for a lot of young people in small towns, they only see as far as their small towns. And there's so much more out there that will never be realized until they search within themselves and their own personal abilities—which I'm still discovering for myself. Sometimes it's scary, but I guess the biggest step is to overcome that fear. Once you do that, it's so exciting. The world is the greatest place. There are a lot of things that go wrong in this world, but that's what builds your character. How you take the mistakes and the problems. That is the very simple message I want to get out to as many people as I can. Even if it means to be happy as a housewife—great—as long as you're happy doing it. It's that simple. It's a simple little message. Get out and do what you want to do.

The question I asked related specifically to Inuit culture, but what's interesting is your message isn't specifically Inuit.

It isn't. That's the thing. It's me—which is what makes it more exciting.

She says through an uncomfortable smile.

My greatest fear when I made the final decision to get into this career was that there were so many things that I was going to have to do that were totally against what might have been traditional 15, 20 years ago. I don't know if I'm emotionally strong enough to take that kind of hassle from my own people. I haven't gotten any yet. If anything, they have applauded me for what I've done. I realize that I didn't give them as much credit as I should have for being open-minded. I have to think of it this way. The European culture, when they came over here, they had to go through change and they still are. That's what's happening to the Inuit people and different Indian groups. We're fighting change. If we can compromise in different areas, and we are, then the change is going to be much easier to take. That doesn't mean our culture and our traditions and our language are going to die. The igloo is an example. Nobody is ever going to live in an igloo again. My mom and dad were born in tents and lived in tents in the summertime, and in igloos in the winter for the first eight or ten years of their lives. If I asked them today, 'Dad, if you had a chance, would you go back to that? Would you want to live in a tent in the summertime?'—no way. In fact, he's probably waiting for me to make my first million so I can build him a mansion. There are things that are going to change that are never going to come back. It's that attitude of change, and accepting change, the attitude that we take into it. That is part of what my people have realized for me, and me for my own career. It's accepting the change for both of us.

You've gone to the world conference on human rights in Vienna. You represented the Canadian Inuit as a spokesperson. Did you want to explain what life was like there? Was that your intention in going?

The intention, as it is today when I go to Europe, is—unfortunately, they have this cute little picture of Eskimo people. They're still living in igloos. In little snow huts. What I wanted to do when I went to Vienna, for those people who understood I was an Eskimo first of all, and Inuit—for them to realize now that we are not what they think we are. I walked in there dressed in what normal European people would wear. I'm not in fur, I'm in your clothing. So that must tell you we're civilized. A lot of people still might think of us as savages or people off the land. That was the biggest thing I wanted people to realize in Europe because—I'm an Eskimo and I don't look savage, do I? This is how we are—we live in your houses, we live with running water, we have bathtubs and showers, all the beautiful stuff you created, we have—and we're used to it. That was all I wanted to do, because I couldn't do any more. Maybe if we do get a tour over there, we'll have more opportunity to speak and to make presentations for them to see more of what we've become. Until then, that was all I could accomplish.

And you're also using the singing to get the word out about your people.

Oh yes, oh yes! You know what? Even if I wanted to avoid it, I couldn't, you know, because unfortunately for the arts and entertainment field, I am an Eskimo and that's the first thing they'll see. If they ask the questions, I will answer honestly. Most of the questions people ask are, like, 'Do you really eat whale blubber?'

Do you?

No. I eat mukduk but that's not whale blubber. Ahh—you won't be grossed out, will you? It's the layer of skin—a layer of skin off the whale. There's a gray layer and then there's the fat. We don't eat the fat, we eat that layer.

It's good, I guess, that you're able to answer these questions in a non-defensive way and understand that people can just be uninformed...as I can be.

As are most people, unfortunately, on the streets in Canada.

Because it's too far away. It's a different culture. And how is one to know....

Until you get the opportunity to ask, you can't.

How different are the concerns of teenagers in the north versus teenagers in the south?

Not at all. It just happens that one is Eskimo and one isn't—one's Inuit and one's Indian and one's black. They're all the same. It's the same as dealing with the issue of abuse. No matter where I go, on an Indian reserve or in a small town in the south, it's still the same. The level of abuse is still the same. It's not different at all. What affects the generation before us automatically affects the generation now and will inevitably affect the younger generation. The cultural differences don't make the problem different. Inuit people deal with the same problems as southern young white people do. You have people in the north with pierced noses with chains going to the ears. It's no different.

The issues that you talk about are, for the most part, so serious. About your people, about change, about sexual abuse. It's very hard. When do you allow yourself to relax? Susan, you're taking a long time to answer this.

Well, I don't, actually. My mind is so used to dealing with it—as a victim myself—having been victimized myself. It was the way I was brought up, in church and always in that mind-state of 'help,' always thinking how to make another change or how to make things easier for these people. The only time I really break away from anything like that is when I'm thinking of a new costume and I'm sewing, or if I'm downstairs in my basement blasting the music. But that's about the only time I'm away from it—and even then, I'm not. You're never really away from your work. I have to accept that.

You're never away from your work?

Never. Never.

People know you as a very serious young woman.

If they could talk to my family, they'd get a totally different picture.

You're concerned with ultimately hoping to create change in the smaller northern section of the world. But how do you deal with bureaucracy and red tape while you're trying to make changes?

I don't. I'll go right over it if I have to. It doesn't stop me. Because for too many years, it did. Again, my dad is an example. People that I've been close to are an example. The Inuit people themselves are an example. I was very offended by a comment that was made by another aboriginal that called aboriginal people passive. It's not fair to dub us as passive people because of the control the government has had over us for so many years. We're not passive—we're forced to be, if we are. That is not a decision we made. And that totally frustrates me. You know what? Red tape, bureaucracy? If I could, I'd just go right over it and right back to my people.

I love the philosophy of that, but practically speaking—everybody wishes that they could jump over the red tape and go for it. How do you deal with it? You've gotten past some things.

I guess it's all in the attitude again. You have to carry yourself in a professional manner, you know. There is a level of professionalism that you have to relate to and understand and do. Once you've reached that level, you can pretty much do anything. People will respect you for what you are and for what you can deliver and provide.

Since you've been speaking on behalf of your people, have you noticed any changes?

In the young people, I have. In the children, I have. They are always the first that are affected, of course, and the first who are disappointed when somebody they look up to falls. But it is the children and the young people who are most affected, and in my work, in *Arctic Rose*, because most of the victims are children, the parents have come along to the show because they've realized this is affecting their children in a real way, like nothing else could. Most parents are government employees. And all the red tape and all the bureaucracy I've ever had to deal with is from the government. It's not something I planned, it's not a strategy to target the children. The target was the abusers. But it's affected the victims. And the parents and the older people who I wanted it to get out to got out through the children. The children were so affected by *Arctic Rose* and the message in there. I guess the whole concept of having a role model—that has affected the parents in the long run. And if you get a family, I think it then affects the whole community.

What's the best advice you've ever received?

It's not so much advice as it is an idea. It comes from B. B. Graham, from the book he wrote called *Hoof Beats*. And it comes from a prophecy in the Bible about the seven forces. But what he said really confirmed for me my way of seeing humanity and seeing people. It became advice for me. He said, 'We create our own catastrophes, we create our own problems. If the world is going to end, it's not because God created it to end, it's because human nature is such that it's making it end. When God created the world, he never created it to end. When God created people he never intended for us to experience pain or heartache. It's because of the way human nature has become.' That is how I decided I had to get into this work or else I would have a lot of anger and look for someone to blame for all the pain and heartache people are going through. Because I'm just as much to blame for the pain and the heartache as other people are. I had to decide one way or the other. Am I going to look for somebody to blame? Or just work with an open mind and know that nobody is to blame for this?

What are you afraid of?

My greatest fear is to let fear control me. That's it. Often my fear is my own personal anger, because I don't think I've dealt with that yet. If you were to ask my parents and my sisters and brothers if they've ever seen me throw a tantrum, I don't think they'd ever say yes, because I never have. Not that I haven't had the urge to throw one. Last night is an example—I had a very close cousin who was 27 when she died. We grew up together. It was the kind of relationship, you know, when you make mud pies, when you collect Barbie dolls, all the stuff you do with your closest friend—that's what she was. She killed herself a year ago. And I was thinking about her last night, and I got so angry. Little things like that. I realized how much anger I have in myself, and I get afraid of that.

Of just letting loose one day?

Yes. Because I will. I guess in my work I can't—or I don't allow fear to control me or the people I work with. We get a lot of calls from abusers and they can be ugly at times when they feel they are being accused constantly because of my music, because of what I speak about.

This is how bad it gets in these communities. I went to have a counseling session in private. The kids ranged from, I think it was seven or eight years old to 17 years old. And their parents didn't know where they were. They couldn't know. The counseling session was done with nobody's knowledge, except for kids and the counselors and myself.

Why do they have to do that?

Because of the abusers.

They will come to the counseling session?

They live with them! They live with the people who abuse them! They can go for a counseling session one evening, go home that night and be abused. Go to the next session, get home, same thing. This is what they live with every day. This is what we deal with all the time.

What's your role in these sessions?

That evening I sang 'Anger and Tears' and they all cried. That's all I did—I sang that song—no music, no nothing, I just sang that song, because that's what they wanted. And all they did was cry. And that's all they could do. I told them, 'All I can say is I know what you're going through.' But I know it's not a lot of help because it is a great deal of emotional turmoil. If I ever am confronted by a very angry abuser or parent, who usually ends up being the abuser, my own anger is so great. If my fear controlled me—I would not want my dad to back down if my abuser approached him. I'd want my dad to take my side. So when I think of it that way—if somebody who calls me and asks me for help ends up having their abuser approach me, I'll fight any way I can. I can't be afraid. I'm not afraid. Because I know. I've experienced that degree of anger and helplessness. So much that you don't ever want to be helpless again.

How would you define success for youself?

I think I've reached it. Success for me is not in the kind of place I live in, it's not the kind of car I drive, it's not in the money I make. As far as I'm concerned, I have reached the highest level of personal success I ever wanted—and that is knowing my limitations, knowing me. I am so happy now for the first time in my life. This is what I wanted to be in the worst way. And finally I am, and I love it. Give me a hug, I'll be happy. I guess if you wanted success in another way—material success—all that I really want to do is give mom and dad what they deserve, for the first time in their lives. Because they've worked so hard. I'd build two houses, attached, so they can live with me and have their own place.

Would they move to the south?

Yes—if I could convince them to do it. I'd want them to be with me.

To end it off...

Already?!

It's three hours! You've been known to say, 'Know who you are, dream your dreams, make a life.' I think it's a fitting way to end the interview if you can explain to me where that came from and how it fits into your life.

I believe that my dad had dreams of a better world. Of a better way. There's got to be a better way. I guess I feel I am accomplishing my dad's dreams in his world. I'm accomplishing my mom's independence. How she would have wanted to be in her own world. I've put the two together and I've become what they both wanted to be. They've never told me that, but I feel I'm a lot like my dad—I've always been told I'm so much like my dad—but I look so much like my mom. So I've got to have both. I guess that need to dream never died. Even though, at the time I was living there, I never felt I would accomplish any of it—I continued to dream. If not for myself, then for my parents, my sisters and brothers. Anybody. Even for myself. Just let me dream. It keeps you alive. Even if it's creating a different world, as long as it's safe. For a lot of victims, it can be a perfect world—even though it's never going to be—it *could* be. It's the most wonderful thing in the world. The ability to dream—because it's such innocence. It depends on how you see it. I can still dream today of a different world, even though I think I've accomplished what I set out to do. I can still dream. I can dream of a child...of a family. Anything. Day by day you've got to have something that keeps you going and dreaming is one of them, for me. It creates a hope. It encourages you to know that there's got to be something out there bigger and better. So I guess that's why I say that.

Severn Cullis-Suzuki

There is an art to being interviewed. It's an understanding of how to respond to a question in such as way as to not offend the interviewer, while very subtly shifting the focus to a subject you're most comfortable with. This skill usually comes after years of having to deal with the media.

Severn Cullis-Suzuki is obviously a very fast learner, because at the age of 14, she handles an interview like a pro. But media is not her passion. Getting her environmentally friendly message out is.

One can say it's in her genes. With activist Nancy Cullis and environmentalist David Suzuki for parents, Severn grew up surrounded by people who believed that change is possible. She also had the privilege of traveling to exotic lands with her parents, meeting the movers and shakers in environmental community. All of this has provided Severn with a unique perspective on the world.

This blue-blooded green lineage that Severn was born into does have a down side, but it comes from a force beyond her control. On several occasions when I mentioned Severn's accomplishments in the context of this book, a cynical remark like "Well, what do you expect, having the connections she does?" was often thrown my way. It bothered me, as I'm sure it does Severn. I can think of hundreds of children born to influential parents who had the potential to initiate change through their inherited fame, but instead chose not to rock the boat. After talking with Severn for two hours (with no prompting from her parents), it was clear that, through her personal commitment and hard work, she is capable of making a difference to our endangered world.

Although she is barely a teenager, Severn's credentials in supporting environmental and human-rights causes are quite astounding. By the first grade she was initiating projects to protect endangered species. Her family's love of nature introduced her to the huge problem of clear-cutting in British Columbia's Stein Valley and the Amazon Rain Forest in Brazil. Before you could yell "Timber," Severn was raising funds to stop the unnecessary carnage. At ten years of age, Severn understood that there was strength in numbers and formed the ECO, the Environmental Children's Organization. Their commitment to fighting pollution and helping indigenous people around the world led to Severn's now famous speech at the Earth Summit in Rio in 1992.

Politicians and environmentalists congregated in Brazil from all over the world, and through perseverance, sheer guts and a little help from her influential dad, Severn Cullis-Suzuki was invited to make her speech in front of the most important environmental policy-makers in the world. Her simple, heart-wrenching plea for respect for the earth and all the children who will inherit it made international headlines and earned her the United Nations Global 500 Award for outstanding commitment to the environment. And to ensure that her message won't be forgotten, Severn has published her speech in a book entitled *Tell the World*, in which she also suggests ways for young people to help our troubled planet.

Severn Cullis-Suzuki is an enthusiastic, articulate future leader who, in the span of a two-hour conversation, made me believe that if she has anything to do with it, the world will be a better place.

Your name is so interesting. What does it mean?

Well, Severn comes from the Severn River in England. My mom was born near a place right by the great Severn River, which is the biggest river in England. When I was born, I looked so Japanese that she wanted people to remember my English roots, too, so she called me Severn. Also because the river was named after a great warrior princess who fought against the Romans and finally, instead of being captured when her army was losing, she threw herself into the river.

Do you celebrate a lot of the traditional aspects of your Japanese ancestry at home?

No, not really. My mom was born in England and she emigrated here when she was six. It was my great-grandparents who emigrated here from Japan, our family is more Canadian than Japanese—we're kind of more English than Japanese, if you know what I mean?

Yes.

My grandparents have moved here, too, and they're pretty Canadian, but no, we don't really celebrate anything Japanese, although both my mom and my dad would like to. They want me and my sister to learn Japanese, and perhaps during the spring break we might go to Japan to learn some Japanese, because my father's writing a book on Japan, but it's only my grandfather who speaks Japanese. My father doesn't.

You mention your grandparents a few times in your book and say you're very lucky to spend a lot of time with them. Do you learn a lot from them?

I'm very lucky that both sets of grandparents live in Vancouver. I only have one grandmother, but my grandparents on my mother's side live right upstairs. When we moved into this house where we're living, my parents couldn't afford it, so they bought it together and now my grandparents live upstairs. It has its drawbacks, but it's really nice, because I can go up and visit them whenever I want. And when our house is in total chaos, their house is always clean and I can go up and take a break. My grandfather, my dad's dad, lives up the hill, so he drops in every now and again. It's wonderful spending time with them because now I'm used to hanging around older people, and my friends aren't. They're not used to hanging around their grandparents and they don't know how to act.

I want to know about your parents. You said that your mom helps with some of your work. Tell me a little bit about the influence that your mom has had on you.

She's been a really big influence. She's just incredible. I think she's wonderful. She's an incredible writer. She used to teach at Harvard. She's a perfectionist. That's kind of a problem sometimes, because when she does something it's done as perfectly as she can get it. But it takes so long to do and, with my dad, he does so many things, but he doesn't spend much time on them. But it's equally as good. So I hope I've inherited half and half—both the qualities. But she's an incredible organizer and she's very, very generous. I don't think I've inherited that part, because she does so many things behind the scenes, for my dad, for myself, and nobody ever gives her credit. But my dad and I, we get all the credit. We get applauded, but she's really the person behind us. I hope one day she will get credited with creating us, because I would never be talking to you right now if it wasn't for her helping me along the way.

What does she do? How does she help you?

She's so determined, and she makes me feel that my ideas are worthwhile. And she helps me organize my speeches and stuff.

Very important part.

She's quite a role model. Because she's a feminist, and she helped me believe that it is possible to do things. She was one of the things that inspired me. When I was younger, when I was about eight or something, she formed her own group. It was a women's group and they contacted the government and asked them if it was okay, so it was official. It was half Native women and half non-Native women and they were trying to help the school system get correct information on Native people in British Columbia, because my sister and I were coming home with all these wrong facts about West Coast Natives, so she was going out and doing all this stuff and I was, like, 'Wow, it's a real organization.' And now she's the executive director of the David Suzuki Foundation, which I think should be called the Nancy Cullis Foundation but then they wouldn't get a lot of money.

Why wouldn't they get money?

Well, because they need a 'name.' The David Suzuki Foundation sounds a little egotistical—that's what I think—but I can see the point. When people think of David Suzuki, they think environment, you know? And so it kind of sums up what the organization is all about.

Yes, I understand.

So, it's both of their organization. It's really doing some neat stuff and she's quite a role model in believing that you *can* do something, and going for it, not just talking about it but doing it. Even if it might take a long time.

I think it's interesting that you call your mom a feminist. I'm curious what your definition of a feminist is.

I'm not sure if I'm like my Mom, but I think she's a feminist in not letting anything stand in her way. I feel she can do anything, and I guess that's kind of a feminist, because women are not really thought of as being able to do anything or—I'm not really sure how to explain it. But my dad considers himself a feminist, too, because he's always talking about this woman power—it's really funny. But I hope I'm like my mom, anyway.

When you say that your mom is a feminist, it's interesting because, for example, when I talk to my mom and she talks about feminism, it was her generation and probably your mom's generation that had to do all those things, like demand equal pay and demand to be allowed to work and not just do the dishes. And then we're born, and when we grow up we kind of expect it. You expect, I'm sure, that if

you want to work, in the environment or whatever you want to do for a living, that you'll be allowed to. Because you're a person first, not necessarily a woman. I think it's our parents' generation that made it possible for us. Do you think of yourself as a feminist?

It depends what you think of as being a feminist. Our teacher asked that in class the other day, and none of the girls put up their hand or maybe there were three people who put up their hands.

I don't think feminism is radical, in terms of what we think today is standard, acceptable to think. It's being equal and having the same opportunities as men. That's what I think. Although I think a lot about other things, I haven't thought of it all that much. I just see my mom as a strong person and I admire her. I think of her as quite an activist for women's rights and aboriginal rights and environmental rights and all these things. She's taken being a woman to her advantage and she's said,'This is what I think as a mother, as a woman' and just speaks from that perspective. Especially in regards to the environment—because she's a mother, she's worried about her children. But I guess you could say that about my dad, too, because that's what my dad does.

Do you get something different from your dad? How is your relationship different with him?

With him? I guess I talk more about sports with him. I don't know why, because my dad was not sportive at all when he was in high school. It was my mom who was captain of every team and the athlete of the year. But I talk about sports with my dad and we talk about different things. I really enjoy talking with my dad, because I take talking with my mom for granted because my mom's always there, but my dad isn't. He travels a lot, so whenever I can see him and we can talk face to face, it's kind of rare. When he's away, I talk to him on the phone and I tell him everything that happens at school. That's the fun thing, I talk to my dad about all my friends and what's happening, and he loves gossip. I tell him about all my friends' problems and all this stuff. I guess it might be good that he goes away, because I enjoy it more.

Your dad is a very well-known and respected research scientist and environmentalist. Both he and your mom are very supportive in helping you reach the goals that you set for yourself. Do you ever encounter cynicism in other people who say that you wouldn't have been able to do what you've accomplished without them?

Yes, I have been asked this question a lot by interviewers—'Don't you think that, if your dad weren't David Suzuki, you wouldn't have been able to do all you're able to do?' And yeah—of course! First of all, I probably wouldn't be as interested in the environment if it weren't for my parents, because they were always involved in different environmental issues and we had a lot of friends. I thought it was exciting growing up with all these problems. I thought it was exciting because we were involved in helping to solve these problems and I've grown up with the sense that you *can* do something if you get together, just because I've grown up in this household. And also because of the doors that dad, a guy like David Suzuki, has opened.

But the thing I always say is that I've taken advantage of these opportunities that have been handed me and sometimes I feel I have a responsibility, because I have these advantages, to go out and do something with it. Like making speeches and trying to get the message out. I've been to every continent in the world except Africa, and visiting all these lifestyles has really opened my eyes. I see my lifestyle in a different kind of way—although I take it for granted a lot of times. But that experience has also changed my ideas. Since I do have an opportunity to see this, and because I have been exposed to environmental issues and I have been shown that I can make a difference, I have a responsibility to go out and do something.

How do you deal with all this attention and keep your head on straight?

Actually, I wanted to slow down this year, because last year I don't think I enjoyed it so much. I got to go to China and I got to go to Japan and got to go all over the place, but it's a lot of work and it's incredibly stressful. The relief after I give a speech, or—not so much interviews, but especially after I give a speech—it's a lot of work, preparing. I get a lot of help from my parents, thank God! Especially my mother. But it is very stressful, and this year I wanted to kind of slow down. I still have school and basketball and my social life. I have friends and I'd like to hang around with them, too. I do, but sometimes it's just too much, and I hope it will slow down. Also, when all these people want to talk to me and I've got offers to be a host on TV and all this stuff, it's just crazy, you know. I'm, like, why? It's incredible, the immediate success I've had. Ever since I gave one speech in Rio, my career—I don't know what you'd call it—the things I've been doing—the rate of it has exploded. I didn't ask for it, it just happened.

So how do you keep your feet on the ground?

I don't know. I just kind of do. I feel like I'm living in two different worlds. I'm two different people. A lot of my friends didn't know about my book—well, they do now, but I'd say all of my friends didn't know I was writing a book until about a month after it was published. They started seeing it in bookstores and started hearing about it. I don't really share it with them because I don't feel it has anything to do with them. I forget about it when I'm with them and I just go to school, and when I come home or when I have to give a speech or something, I concentrate on that. It's kind of hard to balance. I do have to mix them up some of the time, because I do have to give speeches or interviews or whatever while I have to do homework.

Wow.

It's kind of complicated.

It is, yes. People have a hard enough time getting through school without this added responsibility.

Well, but I don't think it's that hard. I shouldn't feel sorry for myself. I'm very lucky that I have been handed this opportunity.

Because your parents are environmentalists, it makes sense that you're aware of the problems that the world population is facing in trying to save the environment. I heard that when you were six years old, your father came home and found you selling his hardcover books for 30 cents.

Well, in Toronto we had so many books, so I just grabbed a whole bunch and I said, 'I'm going to raise money for the environment.' I didn't have an issue, just the environment, and I started selling books. I got in a bit of trouble for that, but it was really funny.

Tell me some other things you did when you were young, when you were seven, eight, nine years old—in your early days of activism.

One example I can give you—we used to live in Toronto when I was really young. This was when I was seven or so. I got together with a bunch of my friends and I said, 'Let's make a parade.' And we had banners saying 'Save the Environment.' We got a whole bunch of these banners and we got all our little brothers and sisters, who were like two years old, and we put them in strollers and we pushed them along, carrying all these flags and we went a whole block. There were about seven little tiny kids walking along with these banners.

Who spelled the word environment?

Oh—I can't remember. We probably had an adult to help us, and cross the street and everything. I remember it was a big thrill having other adults saying, 'Good for you!'

I haven't thought about that for a long time, and I don't really consider that as a time I decided I had to do something. But our family had shown me that it was important. I didn't know any of the details, but I knew I had to do something. I knew the basics—that trees were being cut down, that animals were becoming extinct, our air was being polluted, and I knew I had to do something about it.

It's a terrifying thought. Did you have nightmares about it?

No, not in my sleep, but I did get scared about it and I still do, because it is very uncertain and it's very frustrating why people don't realize the obvious or even—well, am I right?

Because I figure, who's right? Corporations who're polluting or clear-cutting or who are causing environmental degradation or the environmentalists? The environmentalists are saying we won't have any more trees in 20 years, and the corporations are saying we will. But if we cut down all our trees and then find out in 20 years that the environmentalists are right, we're in trouble. But if we save the trees and find out in 20 years the environmentalists were wrong, it's no big deal. We can still cut down those trees. We still have the option to go back. But if we cut down all the trees now, we don't have that option.

How has your approach to environmentalism changed from, say, the time you were 11 years old? That's when you were really becoming involved, right? Now you're 14—big difference, three years—has your approach or attitude changed?

I think the major change came when I was seven—doing that protest and stuff—and then when I was about ten or 11, somewhere in there. Because I realized quite quickly, when I started getting together my own organization, that it wasn't as simple as that. It wasn't—I hate using this term, because everybody uses it—but it wasn't black and white. It wasn't so simple. It was a lot more complex than I had imagined it to be. To try to do something, like help save a bunch of trees or some animals, you had to go through all these complications. You had to raise money. You couldn't just give it to the forest. You had to find out all these little details, and it was a lot harder, so I had to learn how to organize for myself for our organization. Perhaps when I realized it wasn't just animals, and trees being cut down, it was people who were suffering, too—and I've said this often in interviews, but I think it's very true—the turning point I had was when I visited the Amazon rain forest. That was when I was about nine years old and we went down into the jungle for about ten days. It was quite a short trip, but it changed my life. It's a long story, how we got to know the people there, but anyway, we went down and when I came back out, I realized there was all this destruction going on around the village where we had stayed. We'd stayed in a village deep in the Amazon jungle—about an hour and a half plane ride over virgin forest to this little village, which was in the middle of nowhere. The only way we could get out of it was by plane—a little tiny plane. As we flew out, I could see the smoke begin to fill the air and I could see that all around the edges of the forest there was fire eating it away. And I realized that it was my friends in the middle of all this and eventually they would be affected by what was going on in the outside world.

Tell me about ECO and how it began.

After I got back from the Amazon, I said to my friends, 'Listen, it's really scary, what's happening. You know, I have friends in the Amazon and they're in danger and we've got to do something.' I felt it was really urgent. We decided to get together. We didn't know all that much about the issues and so we decided to get educated about them and maybe as a group we might find some solutions and generate more ideas about how we might be able to help.

Sort of like strength in numbers.

Right. We'd support each other. So we started enterprising. We thought, 'We need a good way to fundraise.' This is how ECO started—I started making all these little things out of Fimo, which is a sort of clay that you work with and then it hardens—you cook it in the oven. I would make these little lizards and everybody loved them. I was in Grade 4 and I sold them for 50 cents. They were very hard to make. Then we started making hundreds of these things—I taught my friends how to make them—and it was like a little assembly line we did. We raised the price and raised the price, and in the end they were $7 and we raised hundreds of dollars that way.

That's amazing.

So we would just do little things like that, but obviously you can't raise thousands of dollars by making little brooches. It took a long time to make each one of them. Then we started having bake sales and selling used books, and we gained the support of a local bank called Vancity, for Vancouver, and it funded a newspaper for us. We only have three issues—I think I sent it to you—but that funded that. We published three educational reports, with help from the EYA, which is another organization in Vancouver that is for youths. We've done a lot of projects with them because they're very experienced. They're a network of teenagers who formed their own organizations. Now, they've all joined hands across Canada and there is a group in Australia. They help each other and have a lot of influence. I know the guy who started it, so with help from them we published newspapers and we get fundraising ideas and it's fun along the way.

You said in the book that when you heard about the summit in Rio, you said, 'I've got to go.' But it took $27,000, and then you had to be accepted to participate in the forum. Someone three times your age would be afraid to take on that challenge. Where do you get your determination and perseverance?

I heard about it about a year or so before the actual conference, and I had the idea that all these environmentalists were going to get together, and I said to ECO, 'This is a good opportunity to get the message of kids across.' Because I suspected there wouldn't be any other kids there and I thought, 'Wow, what an impact it would be if we could go as the only kids there'—because it would be outrageous if there weren't any kids. You see, decisions were going to made—really important decisions about what was going to be done. And we thought it would be outrageous if there weren't going to be any kids, because we're going to be the most affected.

Yes. But where do you get this determination and perseverance?

I think I got that because—well, we were very young, and I hadn't learned yet that there was something that I couldn't do. You know, kids can do anything—they think they can do anything—so it was just, like, 'Okay, we're going to go down to Rio—we are!' The reaction we got from our parents was, 'Sure, you go to Brazil—now run along.' It was such a crazy idea. About a year later—because I think I told them about it two years earlier—I said, 'Remember that conference I told you about? It's still on, and I think we should go.' We ran into some group problems, because there were some kids who said, 'Are you crazy? We're never going to go to Brazil.' Looking back, I can see how blind I was. I just knew we were going to get down there and we were going to speak in front of all these world leaders. It was actually very different when I did get down there from what I had imagined. I think, on the whole, it was incredible luck that we were heard. We were just four Canadian kids who were 12 years old, and there were millions of people down there. Delegates, politicians, plus people from all over the world. And four Canadian kids are going to get heard?

We weren't even part of the Canadian delegation or anything, so it was one incredibly lucky thing that happened after the other. One important person happened to be in our audience at one speech. See, what we had to do was get heard—and to get heard we had to give all these little speeches wherever we could. So once my dad gave us an opportunity to speak at a conference, because when he realized that we were going to go down, and when my parents realized I was serious, then they started helping and taking me seriously, and helped us to get down there. Without my mom's help and continual support, there's no way I would have gotten down there. No way.

You've been asked in other interviews if you would consider a life in politics, and you said no. But you also said you wished politicians would stand up for what they believe in. Why wouldn't you get into politics when it seems you have good qualities and ideals that most politicians don't? This is your calling.

A lot of people have told me that. They've said, 'Oh, you should become a politician.' Actually, about a month ago I was really interested in becoming a politician, and—have you ever heard of Jim Fulton?

No.

Oh, well—he was a politician in Ottawa and he is now part of the board of the David Suzuki Foundation. He is one of the most normal persons in politics that I've known, and he did some pretty radical things. It's quite exciting and I found it inspirational and I thought, 'Wow, I can't believe that a politician could do that.' Things like—there was this dam that was going to stop some salmon getting upstream at Capilano. There was this centuries-old stream that was going to be stopped and all these salmon would die, and he went there and there was this huge salmon that was dying. He picked it up, put it in his jacket, got on a plane to Ottawa and went into this big conference with it down his pant leg. In the middle of someone's speech who was saying, 'Everything's fine and this dam won't cause any damage,' he pulled out this fish and slapped it down in front of this person and said, 'Oh yeah?' I think that's inspirational and I'd like to be someone who'd do that, but I don't think, being a woman, it would have as much impact.

Why?

I don't know. For some reason I can't see a woman doing that. But I'd love to do it.

I'm so shocked! I can't believe you're even saying that. Why? Do you think politicians perceive women differently than men?

Actually, my dad said this, and I have to agree. I think women have to become men to achieve in politics. They have to forget about all their maternal instincts—the emotional part of being female. You have to hand it to politicians. I think it's a hard job and I don't think you can please anyone. I'm beginning to realize that there are so many people out there who could think I'm this bratty kid—who am I to be telling all these big leaders we have to change our ways? I've only been around 14 years—I'm not living in a poor family. I have everything I need handed to me, and who am I to tell people we should give things up or change? Just the thought of having a few enemies is awful—I hate it. So I can't imagine being a politician, because politicians have so many enemies. When you stand up for anything, you're always going to have enemies and that's one of the things, one of the big drawbacks. I think that's why a lot of people don't say anything.

I think a lot of people have a very negative view of our generation. The slackers, the loafers. That they're greedy. Do you agree with that?

Yes. Actually I do. Because this generation is the result of every generation working really hard to create a good lifestyle. I don't know how to explain it. These are good questions. I think Canadians have a very good standard of living. This generation especially takes it for granted, because we don't have to work as hard as our parents did. The standards in education and technology are getting higher. You know how there're these stories about 'When I was a child, I had to walk six miles in the snow,' and you get the impression that your parents had to work a lot harder than you do and I think it's kind of true. This is one thing that my grandparents have taught me, the things we completely take for granted. In the olden days, when they were young—it took effort to communicate, to make the new kind of technology function. It took a lot of effort and I think that's one of the reasons that kids today may be thought of as greedy. It's because we don't have a sense of reality. We take so much for granted. That's one of the reasons I may see things differently than other kids might. It's because I have had the chance to travel to poorer countries and I have had just a glimpse of the other kinds of lifestyles people live. I can never—having seen the situation in Rio, you know, the street children—I could never even begin to compare my life with that of another kid my age who's living on the street. I can't even begin to imagine what it's like. I take a lot for granted myself. What I hope what all Canadians will do—I think this will really help, I think this is one of the biggest steps we have to take in the right direction—is looking around ourselves and not taking so much for granted.

Being happy with what we have?

Exactly. That way we won't want to suck so many of the resources out of other countries and want to consume, consume and want more and more. We have to look at what we already have, and be thankful.

Is that your first rule as an environmentalist?

Probably. A lot of people have said, 'What can we do?' I always say we have to get educated about the problem and change the way we think.

What would you recommend to someone for a good education in the environment?

A lot of people would say you could read books or you could contact environmental groups. I think one of the best ways we can get a sense of what the problems are—the kind of weight the environment carries—is by talking to our elders.

Tell me about your own elders. Explain to me how life was different for them.

Not only my elders. My family has spent a lot of time with West Coast Natives, my dad's been adopted into several families, and I've been exposed to that kind of knowledge. The West Coast Indians still value their elders, and the elders know how to tell stories. Especially in that culture, you can see how radical the changes have been in their lifetime. It wasn't that long ago that Canadian Indians were living as they had for thousands of years. So they can tell us the changes that have happened. Also they have felt the change environmentally, with the trees cut down, they feel the loss more than we do, because they're so attached to the land. I think I've learned from that. I've learned the value of the land. It's more than just land. You're a part of it, you're attached to it. Especially the aboriginal people, who have lived on this land for thousands of years.

Let's look ahead to when you're, say, 25. And let's say you're going to go into the field of marine biology. Considering what's happening to the rivers and oceans these days,

what sorts of problems do you see yourself facing as a marine biologist?

Well, pollution is obviously one of the big problems. That's one of the reasons why I want to be a marine biologist, to be exposed to all those wonderful creatures in the ocean and to the wonderful mysteries and maybe, perhaps, make a difference. It's important that you fight for what you love and for what's close to you.

What about you as a teenager? What about you as a person who's just trying to have some fun in your life? What about peer pressure and the fact that I'm sure a lot of people, in high school for example, would perceive you as a goody two-shoes, you know, who's always doing the right thing? How do you deal with that?

Well, you see, that's another problem with being—with getting up and saying things publicly. People have to know who you are. I can't be anonymous any more.

I can relate. Speaking about dealing with being a teenager, what's your take on drugs?

People are always talking about peer pressure and don't let your friends convince you to do things. I think we're all strong enough to say no to that kind of thing, or to do what we want to do—if that's your choice, do it. The thing with drugs is you're getting away from reality. If you have a problem, you have to deal with it. I have so many things, little problems that are in the back of my mind, and I try to push them away as much as possible, by doing other things, and so it grows and the problem's worse. That's one of the scary things about drugs. Not the immediate effect, but the long-term effects of trying to push away reality and trying to hide behind that, because you just get deeper and deeper into the cycle.

Yes. You know what shocks me? It's that you're 14 years old. No matter how smart you are, you've only lived for 14 years, and yet you have such insight. How did you figure that out?

Oh, I don't know. I have pretty strong ideas about things, but I hope I'm open-minded enough to change those ideas or be open to other opinions, because that's the only way you can learn.

What's the best advice you've ever been given?

Well, my mom has always said, 'Keep it simple, stupid.' That applies in writing, and in math and it also applies to getting your message out. If you want to get your message out, keep it simple, straightforward and to the point. If you only have five seconds to get your message out, or if someone asks you, 'What is your message?' then you're going to want to get it across in as few words as possible so that it sticks in people's minds.

It also applies to environmentalism in general. If you keep your life simple, it's better.

If your life was simpler, you'd be happy. People are always saying technology has made our lives so much better, but technology makes us take on even more, so we're busier. There are just more efficient ways of doing a hundred things at one time. I don't think the businessman in New York is very happy. A lot of the environmentalists are saying right now that we don't have to drastically change our way of living, we don't have to lower the standards. We want to simplify it so we can make our standard of living higher. I don't think people living in this world right now are happy.

If you were given three wishes for how people should treat Mother Earth, what would those three wishes be?

Humans are incredible creatures—we're flying off into space—and now we're saying we have to help save the environment, which is a problem we created ourselves. Maybe one of my wishes would be that people could realize the problem and agree with each other enough to find some kind of solution. That's why I'm sad. The conference in Rio was supposed to be like that. Even though a lot of people are dissatisfied with the results that came out of it, most people knew that incredible, spectacular things weren't going to come out of that conference. But I think all those people getting together was one big step in the right direction. At least now the environment isn't an imaginary problem. It's real enough for the biggest heads of state to get together and that's a step in the right direction.

Okay. So your number one wish would be for people to agree that there is a problem and to start working together to find a solution. Number two?

Throughout the history of man, we've always worked so that we could develop what we call a higher standard of living, but we've made it more complicated, with more and more technology. It's called progress, but then again, it's caused a lot of corruption and a lot of discontent. So perhaps my second wish would be for it not to be in human nature to always want to climb the next step, to always be one step higher, because it complicates our lives.

And number three. This is your final wish. You've worked really hard for this. You've talked to me for two hours.

I've thought—I wish the environment was covered in trees. All around if there were trees, you know, no city or anything. Not everyone would be happy. So if there was a rule that everyone had to be happy, it could just work itself out—I don't want to be bothered with the details, but if everybody could be happy...if you think about it, it sounds really simple, but what more would you want, if everybody was happy?

But what would you do with all your time? You'd have nothing to fight for.

Maybe there would be little battles, to occupy you, or something.

Maybe you'd have time to do your homework.

Exactly. May I just say something? One of the reasons that I am speaking out and that I did write the book is because maybe other kids will say, 'Hey, that could be me. I should try to speak out too.' You know, I'm not so alone. I think more and more kids are getting worried. So it is more important to get their voices and there are going to be more and more kids out there who are concerned about the environment.

Sarah McLachlan

I knew there must be justice in the world after my interview with Sarah McLachlan. As we sat down in a hotel lobby for our lunch-time chat, Sarah's career was exploding all around her. Not only was her Canadian tour selling out at the speed of light, but more dates had to be added due to the incredible demand.

According to the last report I had heard, Sarah had sold out four consecutive nights in Toronto (a feat even most international artists can't do) and her latest album was topping the sales charts. Sarah has become one of Canada's most popular performers, but the adoration she's feeling from her fans is very different from her experiences growing up in Halifax. Sarah was one of those teenagers who never felt that she fit in. She saw herself as an outsider all through high school and didn't really feel happy. Today, the opposite is true. Sarah has earned her happiness and, with it, a new sense of confidence.

I went through a lot of the same things that Sarah did when I went to high school and I empathize with her feelings of somehow not ever being good enough. It seems that those of us who have to work harder in developing ourselves during our teenage years have the potential to end up with strong, unique and non-conformist personalities, all of which I feel are important for personal and professional success.

When Sarah McLachlan was growing up, her parents recognized her innate musical aptitude. Classical piano and voice lessons came soon after. She eventually gave them up when she realized that her artistic vision was more contemporary and free-form than her teachers were willing to accept. At the age of 17, performing her first gig with a new-wave band in Halifax, she was discovered by Nettwerk Records, a new Vancouver record label. Her parents discouraged her from signing a record contract at this point because she hadn't even finished high school. When that day did come two years later, Sarah's bags were packed and she was on the next plane to the opposite end of the country. Later that same year, based in Vancouver, she released her debut album, *Touch*. Since then she's recorded *Solace* and most recently, *Fumbling Towards Ecstasy*, her most successful album release yet.

Reaction from her fans is intense. She is beloved. Her voice is haunting, her music sophisticated and sublime. Women can relate to songs that are romantic and strong, poetic and intelligent. And almost every man I know sighs and becomes dreamy-eyed when Sarah's name is mentioned. However, it's more than her music and looks that invite such fan loyalty. After several years of soul-searching and wondering where she fits in, Sarah is finally comfortable in her own skin. Her story exemplifies the simple truth that you should go after what you believe.

If you do this, then you're following the same path to happiness that Sarah McLachlan has discovered.

When I look at you, I see a strong woman who is dealing with her success. What do you see?

Oh, well. This is too deep. I see quite a happy person. On most days, I think, an attractive, vivacious person.

Gosh. Is this a new thing, being happy?

Yeah, definitely. In childhood and adolescence especially, I had a lot of trouble, the typical parent stuff, where I wanted to be my own person but I had no idea what that was. I was brought up in quite a strict family and my parents' ideals and my parents' moralities were definitely projected onto me. I don't feel I was much of an individual. I had a low self-esteem. I could never figure out why—I always seemed fine, to me. But, well, a classic story—in Grade 6, a girlfriend and I showed each other our bodies—she had breasts. I didn't yet, so I was quite fascinated. And somehow the story leaked out and—it's so funny, these little things that completely shape one's life. This story leaked out in Grade 7 and I was having a good time in Grade 7. I actually had friends for the first couple of months and I actually had a boyfriend and had my first kiss and everything. But this story spread and all of a sudden my name was dragged through the mud. Everyone started calling me Medusa all the time and all the boys who passed through the hallways would fall down on the ground and start screaming and writhing. I was terribly upset and I cried and cried, which was exactly the reaction they wanted. Curiously enough, the other girl, who was very well off and well respected—her name never got mentioned. It was always just me, because I was going to a fairly upper-class school—everybody was very well off and I was very middle class. I didn't have four alligator T-shirts on at a time.

Thank God!

They would layer them! Just a show of their wealth, you know. They were $40 apiece. It was a big deal to have one, and by God I had to have one. I begged my mother forever because that would mean I would fit in. It didn't do it, obviously. So needless to say, my self-esteem was in my little toe for a number of years and then I guess in Grade 10 or 11, I started hanging out with the punk rockers, the social rejects.

The ones who didn't fit in?

The ones who didn't fit in.

I was in that crowd, too.

All of a sudden I got accepted, and guys started liking me again, and I was semi-normal, to those people, but to nobody else.

Would that be the more artistic, creative people?

Yes, some of them were. A lot of them just didn't have anything. A lot of them were from poor families. It seemed like they were lost souls and we all converged in this lost-souls community.

This was in Halifax?

Yes. On the front steps of QEH—that's the high school I went to. My parents had an absolute fit. I wasn't allowed to go around with any of these people, so I started lying. I walked around with this huge guilt complex for years because of it. But you know, my mother and I have dealt with this stuff now. I'm an adult and she's an adult and so we can talk about stuff on a friendship level and I say, 'Yeah, I was awful to you and you were awful to me,' and we can admit that to each other now. It was tough, because I wanted so much to fit in and my mother wouldn't believe me. She would always tell me, 'You're so beautiful, you're so talented, how could people not like you?' But when I think about it, I had no self-esteem, so how could anybody else like me?

I may be wrong, but women of your mother's generation, our parents' generation, had a very different upbringing than us. It was probably bad for the husband if the woman had good self-esteem because she might demand things that he couldn't or wouldn't want to give her.

Yes. But it seems that whole age of women and men in general were brought up to ignore their bodies and ignore what their bodies were telling them. To me, if you're not in touch with your body, you're not in touch with yourself. Your emotional, physical and mental states are so interconnected. But my mother's generation didn't talk about it.

There seems to be more of a sisterhood now, in our generation.

Yes. Totally.

Girls get together, and we talk. We sometimes talk about things that make you blush, but we realize that we're all going through the same sorts of things.

It's such an important thing. Talking is therapy. It's like letting your voice become solid. Like sending it out and having someone answer back. And saying they've been through the same thing, it's like kindred spirits. If nobody ever says anything, then communication gets closed down and nobody ever learns anything.

The question that I originally asked you was...

Oh— yeah!

You're happy now. You were talking about why you weren't, and now you are, so ultimately, what happened to make you a happy person?

Well, an awful lot of things. But the most important thing to me is—I got a record contract when I was 19 and I had no idea that would ever happen to me. I would probably never have gone searching for it, it came to me. I totally believe in karma and I believe that this was a chance so I totally took that and decided, 'Well, I can fail or I can work really hard and try to make this work.' I also have to say that I was so incredibly lucky to get a record contract with a company that allowed me to discover who I was. I had no idea what kind of person I was, much less what kind of musician I wanted to be. And Nettwerk gave me the contract. They set me up in a studio. They said to write songs. They did not channel me, they did not push me in any direction. All they gave me was support.

That's an anomaly in the industry?

Yes! All they did was nurture me. Wherever I wanted to go, they let me explore that avenue, and then they put out my first record. At that point, I was quite excited, but at 19 years old I never thought about any of the stuff I think about now. My mind seems to work very slowly in rationalizing and dealing with situations. A lot of stuff goes by me very fast and then, maybe in six months I'll have a week off and it all comes to the surface. As if your body tells you, 'Now you have the time to deal with this—here I come.' Every Christmas, I get sick because I have five days off, so there's my time to get sick. I don't have time to get sick any time else.

You have an incredible voice. What talents were you born with?

Voice, definitely. I've always been able to draw. And I've always been able to sing. The guitar and the piano, and instrumentation, I took lessons. Long before I started taking piano lessons, I would sit down at the piano and pick things out. I played things off the radio. I had quite a good ear to pick up the stuff, but the lessons definitely helped. They gave me something much beyond just being able to pick something up by ear. They gave me a great knowledge of chord structure and melody and harmony and that definitely helped in writing songs. Although when I started writing, I picked from a classical background and tried 15 chord changes. You know, apiece. Then I realized, no Sarah, this is a pop song—three chords, c'mon let's get simple here.

So you knew too much?

Or I was bogged down by some of that knowledge. It was a hindrance. I certainly would not say that I knew too much, because I got what I needed out of the classical music years before I stopped taking lessons. I was interested up to a certain point and then after that, it just became monotonous. I didn't feel like I was learning anything else, partially because of my teachers, because I had simply lost interest, because it became very strict. I got to a point where, 'Okay, I like playing this piece, but now I'm going to start improvising' and I could not do that in class. It's not cool. It's like military, you know? And I was, like, 'Relax. I want to feel it, I want to do it this way. This feels right.' 'Well, it's got nothing to do with feeling right.' I've always fought against that. I've been instinctually driven since I was born, and that's the only thing that keeps my head above water.

What part did your parents play? Did they push you to take classes or did you push them to allow you to take classes?

The great thing about my parents is, from the point when I was four years old, they saw that I had this talent—that I could draw and that I was interested in music so they shipped me off to piano lessons and Saturday morning art classes at the art college. They totally supported me. But those lessons were all quite expensive. They were mostly private lessons and so, six or seven years in, I hit adolescence and they decided, 'Okay, we've invested all this money and we want you to keep going.' Knowing that they didn't want me to have a career in it, they just wanted me to be a classical musician. They knew there was no money in a music career unless you were in the top ten, which is very, very hard. And they knew I wasn't about to practice ten hours a day on something that I wasn't passionate about. My passion was pop music. I'd listen to the radio and learn all the songs by ear and play them. But I kept taking lessons until I was about 16 or 17.

You talk about having had low self-esteem yet you are so driven, so headstrong. There is a confidence there.

My mother gave me that. It's a reaction against what she was. She always says, 'You never learned anything from me, you only took my bad traits.' And I say, 'I took your bad traits and I ran with them, I tried turning them around.' It's like she showed me what I didn't want to end up like. That's a sad thing to say, but she gave up everything to marry my father and to put him through school and to raise all the kids. The greatest thing now is that about seven years ago she decided to go back to school. She's finished her master's degree. Now she knows what it's like to have a taste of freedom. And I'm, like, 'Right on, mom!'

Do you think you've had an influence on her?

Maybe my leaving inspired her. I was the last one to leave, and in a sense it was a kind of betrayal, because I had to get away. I was completely mirroring my parents and I had to get away to discover who I was, so I had to leave home and move away. That was really hard on her because I was leaving her.

Were you leaving her?

I was leaving 19 years of memories that I wanted to get away from, but I was so excited by Vancouver, because nobody knew who I was and I could start fresh. In a sense it was almost dangerous, because I could adopt any personality I wanted and be that, because no one knew who I was, but you know, my own personality reared its ugly head and there was no getting away—I am who I am. But once again, I was incredibly lucky to wind up with a group of people who were supportive emotionally, and financially for that matter, at the start. I feel so blessed because of that and I feel I should give some of that back. I mean, I feel as a human being we have that responsibility. What you get from people and what you want to give with your music. I get so much comfort and caring from music that I want to give that back out. Almost like a sharing thing. Again, it's communication, it's therapy. Everything that goes into my songs is stuff that needs to come out of me. It's questions I'm asking, and whether or not I find the answers doesn't really matter, it's that I'm searching for it and may be coming a little bit closer. If I can share that with other people...I didn't realize that's what I was doing until I started getting all the letters from people saying how strongly my music had affected them. A wild story that I like to tell: The first show in Vancouver, a woman wrote me a letter saying that her daughter had died in a car accident with two of her best friends the year before. One of the things she had in common with her daughter was my music and she asked me—she was going to be at the concert—she asked me if I would play 'I Will Not Forget You' and dedicate it to these three girls. So I did, and I met her after the show and she was really emotional and she was crying and shaking, and I started crying, and we held each other for five minutes. That night I had this beautiful crystal, it was very shiny and smooth, and I had it in my hand all night. So I said, 'Here, take this. I'd like to give you this. This gives me a lot of strength. I hope it gives you some strength.' And I gave it to her, and we talked for a while, and a little while later I left. I went out the backstage door and I met this Japanese fellow who'd been waiting outside and he said, 'I'm from Japan and I'd like to start relations between Japan and Canada with the music industry' and stuff. We talked about it and then he said, 'I'm a Buddhist, and I don't know what your belief is, but I'd like to give you this ring,' and he said, 'This is my fate, this is my strength, and I'd like to give it to you.' It was total, intense karma. I get goose bumps every time I tell the story.

You gave, and it came back to you...the karma.

Yes. Total karma.

Have you read the book *Generation* X?

Lately, actually I did.

There's a lot of people who're talking about this book—using it like a catch phrase.

I'd like to think that it's generalizing too much and that there're lots of other kinds of people out there in our peer group than those kinds of people, who are over-educated and jaded, too young. Who think there are no good jobs left and are all incredibly vain. They don't sound like very pleasant people to be around. I know some people like that and they bore me. I may find them entertaining for about half an hour, but it's all a facade. They're like actors.

Would you define yourself as a feminist?

I think the bottom line, the simplest thing, is that I want to be treated as an individual and I want to be treated as an equal. Not necessarily just to men but to women as well. I don't know the terminology, but I think I'm more of a humanist than anything else. Men have gone through a lot as well as women, and especially, you know, with the feminist thing, there's this whole backlash of men-haters—men are bastards, men are pricks. We're all trying to fight the same battle, but we have to fight it in different ways because of the different things that have led us towards it, the different kinds of social stigma. I love people. I've never understood the social differences between—you're a girl so you can't do this, or he's a guy so he can't go here or he's black so he can't go here. All that stuff. It's prejudice.

What about politics? Does that play any part in your life?

I know nothing about politics. Nothing. The little that filters into my life always seems ugly, for the most part. It seems like it's based on an awful lot of bullshit and it's a scary thing isn't it? These people are running our country.

You're in a position of power. You're standing up before probably a couple of thousand people who are there to listen to you. Do you use your platform?

I use my platform for what I feel comfortable with. Every single individual has different goals and different reasons for being in this world and different purposes, and I have geared my life towards defining my purpose, which, to me, is being a better person and having a sense of responsibility towards myself and towards everyone else around me. I also truly believe that if I am happy and if I can share that lightness with other people, if I can give other people that happiness, then somehow that might count for a little bit in their lives and give them a little more clarity. And vice versa—I love it when people write letters and say how the songs have affected them. It makes it clearer to me.

When you look back at the records you were making at 17, 18 or 19 years old what were you writing about then? And what are you writing about now?

I've always been writing about relatively the same thing—it just evolves. I'm allowing myself to go deeper into myself each time. I was always writing about emotions and sort of a day in the life of. At first I felt I had absolutely nothing to say. I was completely a product of my parents at that point. So I had to figure out who I was. I think that first record was an amazing trip into myself. Just start the ball rolling and figure out my own identity. And then, with *Solace*, I'd been out on the road for a year. I was a little wiser and I'd started to see things outside of my own little world. Like with 'Shelter.' I saw a vivisection tape. I was in Nettwerk and Skinny Puppy was there. They were watching this footage and I just freaked. It floored me. I was, like, 'What is this?' And he said, 'Let me tell you what's going on in the world' and it was one of those little things that explode in your brain.

It's unbelievable how much we don't know.

Oh, it's true. For me, where I am now, I live my life fairly cocooned, especially when I'm out on the road, because it's such an intense job for me to sing every night. I want to do the best job I can and I need to be so focused, because I'm distracted so easily that I feel that I almost have to go through life like this sometimes, just to keep my own identity and my own self really strong. Out here, there're all these people giving me all this adulation every night, telling me how great I am. I really have to say, 'Thank you, yes, I know you think I'm great, but what do I think about me?' I have to remember who I am, for myself.

Does that come out in the lyrics in *Fumbling Towards Ecstacy*?

Yes. Definitely. One of the greatest experiences in my life—well, two great experiences. One of them was going to Thailand and Cambodia last year with World Vision and Terry David Mulligan. The focus was AIDS and prostitution and poverty in these countries and what I saw was incredibly shocking. You see a lot of stuff on television and you're desensitized to it. When you're over there, you can't turn away, because it's in your face 24 hours a day and you're forced to deal with it.

So how did you get involved?

The focus of World Vision was the Year of the Woman/Child, so they wanted a woman artist and they also wanted someone who was of my generation. They thought that I would be someone who my peers would listen to. In a sense that was my first real experience being a spokesperson for my generation. It was not something I felt terribly comfortable with, but at the same time it was an amazing opportunity and I really wanted to go. I thought it would be a great thing for my life and a great thing for my art. And it turned out that it was. It really rocked my world. I was horrified by the cruelty in the world, and in the fact that these people simply have nothing. But at the same time, a lot of these people who have nothing are—they have nothing material, but they have so much spiritually. So I was left trying to figure out, 'How does it relate to my world?' It made me feel incredibly blessed and lucky. For a long time it was like, 'I really can't complain, you know.'

The other important thing was being alone for seven months making this record. Being away from everything I was comfortable with, everything that I knew, except for my cats, I had to bring them. That time of solitude was amazing. Amazing time to make me really, really strong, because I'd gone through a year and a half of being on the road, I'd gone through the documentary shooting of that film, but everything was moving by so quickly. Then I took the time to stop. With me, like I said, it takes a while, it slowly seeps out. That time alone was amazing to work things out. It was really hard, because I'd never been by myself and my brain was sort of eating itself because I had nobody to talk to. Usually I'm around my friends and we just vent on each other. I think when you're dealing with anything about yourself, you are completely alone. There's nobody who can figure it out except you. So that time gave me incredible strength. And then songs just started coming out really easily and I hardly edited them at all. They would come out in three hours or three days, where before it would take months to finish a song. Full pieces would just burst. It was like a birthing thing—it just came out of me.

What was the best advice you ever received?

Believe in yourself. Find out what it is you believe in and believe in it.

Who told you that?

Pierre Marchand. My producer. My guru.

And what would be the best advice you'd pass on to someone?

The same thing. Very simple words. It's one of the questions that the band Sloan asked me, in Halifax, before they were signed. They said, 'What should we do?' And I said, 'The most important thing is find out exactly what the reasons are, search inside yourself for the reason you're doing this, the real reason, and know it, so that when all these people come at you, wanting to pull you in different directions, you make sure you know what you want to do, and try and stick with that as best you can. Believe in that because that's why you're here.'

You've become a role model, how do you feel about it and how do you deal with it?

I think I have a responsibility as a human being to be the best I can be, for myself first and foremost, and if I'm like that, I think I can be a fairly good person for other people around me. I think that's pretty good.

To put it into perspective—ultimately this book is going to be read by, I hope, a lot of young women who look up to you. Are you comfortable with that?

I'm getting more comfortable with it as I get more comfortable with myself. If I wasn't happy with myself, then I wouldn't want anybody looking up to me, but I'm pretty happy with the way my life's going and I'm pretty confident that I'm doing things for the right reasons. So I don't mind people looking up to me then, because I believe in what I'm doing and therefore it's okay for other people to believe in me.